READY, SET,
Cooperate

Also in the Ready, Set, Learn series:

Ready, Set, Read and Write

Ready, Set, Count

Ready, Set, Explore

READY, SET,
Cooperate

Marlene Barron

with
Karen Romano Young

A Skylight Press Book

John Wiley & Sons, Inc.
New York • Chichester • Brisbane • Toronto • Singapore

To my grandchildren, Sarah, Alexander, and Benjamin

—M.B.

For Kim and Matthew with love and thanks

—K.R.Y.

Illustrations by Elaine Yabroudy.

This text is printed on acid-free paper.

Published by John Wiley & Sons, Inc.

The publisher and the author have made every reasonable effort
to ensure that the experiments and activities in the book are safe when
conducted as instructed but assume no responsibility for any damage
caused or sustained while performing the experiments or activities in this
book. Parents, guardians, and/or teachers should supervise young readers
who undertake the experiments and activities in this book.

Library of Congress Cataloging-in-Publication Data

Barron, Marlene
    Ready, set, cooperate / Marlene Barron with Karen Romano Young.
        p. cm. — (ready, set, learn series)
    "A Skylight Press book."
    Includes bibliographical references and index.
    ISBN 0-471-10275-X (pbk. : alk. paper)
    1. Child development. 2. Interpersonal relations—Study and teaching
(early education). 3. Early childhood education—Parent participation.
4. Early childhood education—Activity programs. I. Young, Karen
Romano. II. Title. III. Series
HQ767.9.B375   1996
305.23'1—dc20   95-36111

Printed in the United States of America

10 9 8 7 6 5 4 3 2 1

Contents

"Only connect! . . . Live in fragments no longer."

E. M. Forster, *Howards End*

Introduction

If you were a postal worker, now and then you'd see a letter addressed something like this: "Main Street, New York, New York, U.S.A., Planet Earth, Solar System, Milky Way." You'd pass the mail along with a smile, knowing that there's another child in the world who's keeping her* sense of humor while trying to figure out where she fits in.

Well, aren't we all trying to answer that question? If you want to help your child ask and answer that question for herself, you've come to the right place. By exploring social studies—civics, geography, history—and the arts, children develop a sense of who they are and where they fit in their family, their school, their town, their world, and even their planet and galaxy.

This book is written for parents of children ages three through seven, give or take a little on either end of the range. It's designed to help you help your child to learn how other people live, to make connections with people of all ages, colors, creeds, talents, and abilities, and to see friends as people with whom to share, learn, and work. Through the activities in this book, you can make the most of these vital years when your child moves from babyhood to childhood, from your lap to formal education, from seeing you as provider and cuddler to seeing you as collaborator and companion.

Some of you may already have a child in school and are looking for ways to foster a love of history, geography, and the arts, to enhance your child's language and problem-solving experiences, to increase his sense of himself, and to help him become more adept at getting along with other children as well as adults. In this book, you'll find activities that work in tandem with your school's approach and make social studies and art a part of daily life at home.

Some of you may have a young child. You'll find ways to use the daily business of family life—whatever you're doing, indoors or outdoors—to give her the best possible base for communicating and connecting with other people, for expressing

* I'll use *he* and *she, his* and *her* interchangeably until the English language evolves a word that means both.

1

herself verbally and artistically, and for understanding how events become stories and then what we call history.

What's the best way to enhance your child's life during this exploratory period? The creators of many materials on the market today would have parents believe that their children are empty vessels, waiting to be filled up with information and skills they "need" to become what some call culturally literate. But what is real cultural literacy if not an understanding of people?

Children are predisposed, by nature and by their motivation, to make sense of their surroundings, to make every attempt to grasp (often literally) everything they see and to learn all they can about it. Children of this age group already know a great deal about how the world works. They understand that everything that lives requires food, shelter, and a way to get around. When it comes to humans, they realize that there are many kinds of food; different types, styles, and sizes of shelters; and numerous ways to get around, from crawling to skateboarding to flying the Concorde to—and is this really stretching the concept of locomotion and transportation?—surfing the Internet.

I firmly believe that children growing up now, the adults of the twenty-first century, will need to be flexible thinkers, good imaginers, and eager acceptors of other people's circumstances. No matter what your child's age, he already knows that humans have plenty in common besides food, shelter, and locomotion. Humans express themselves through language, music, art, or dance; they clothe themselves for warmth (and for style); and they get together to celebrate. Your child is ready to move ahead to talk about these matters, to observe, explore, create, and experiment with them, to find things that people have in common and to understand the differences.

As Head of a Montessori school in New York City and a longtime specialist in early childhood education, I've seen children fall in love with social studies—the study of people and cultures—in a natural way. The ones who experience the most success, who express their needs, interests, and passions, and who appreciate similar expressions in others (those in the room with them, those on the other side of the world from them, and those whose time has passed) are the children whose early years were spent being respected and learning to respect the other children and adults around them—in as many situations as possible.

This book will show you ways to encourage your child to open her mind and heart to what's inside others—any day, in any situation. I have gathered and developed these fun, challenging activities during a quarter of a century of teaching and observing the growth of young children, so I know that they work—and that you and your child will enjoy doing them.

While the book gives you step-by-step instructions for each activity, the activities are open-ended. This means that you can make them your own, use them as starting points, change them as you go along, and end up with a different outcome each time. Through these activities you can create the kind of environment that gives your child plenty of opportunities to learn. What's more, you can use these activities to take advantage of the opportunities that arise all around you and your child—on television, in books, in conversations, in stores, even in your own closet. The sixty activities here actually become hundreds of activities when you see them as models for ways to think about social studies with your child. For example, Activity 1: The Grandparents of Pajamas, is a study of what people wear and used to wear to sleep in at night. Why not take the same basic plan and apply it to underwear, shoes, toilets, or vehicles?

Each activity is designed to help you give your child experience with different aspects of history, geography, art, the community, and more. The goal of each activity is to help your child see in some way how he might fit in the world, and how others fit there too. Everything you need is here: a list of materials, step-by-step instructions, and an explanation of the activity's purpose. Built into each activity are ideas for developing the activity further as your child moves ahead (over a day, weeks, or years), for extending it into other areas, and/or for using it with more than one child.

I'm willing to bet that most of these activities will help you become more involved with your child and more confident of her natural abilities and talents. You might not use every activity. You might not use an activity more than once. But do try everything. Make changes to suit your needs and your child's needs. Make the activities your own. The goal is to make iden-tifying, investigating, and experimenting with issues in social studies and the arts a beloved and comfortable process for you and your child to share.

Educational Philosophy: Why These Activities Work

Below, I've outlined some of the general ideas that you'll find running through the activities.

Whole Learning

My approach to the process of learning about cultures —other cultures, our own large culture, and the individual cultures of community, neighborhood, classroom, or family—is called *whole learning*. It incorporates all the ways we observe, communicate, and categorize the information we gather to make meaning of the world. Meaning-making happens every time a person holds a conversation, hears a song, looks at a painting, or listens to a story—whether based in fact or fantasy—about the world. The more a child learns about people, places, and things, the more he puts two and two together to see how a situation got the way it is, what people have to do with the situation, and how people might change it in the future.

How do you teach your child about the vital importance of food to individuals, societies, and cultures? You don't need to. She already knows a great deal about it. As a newborn baby, she naturally sought out milk. It wasn't long before you provided solid foods, and not long again before she started reaching out for anything that looked edible. She learned—through some trial and error—the difference between food and non-food, and as she grew, she learned about different foods every day. As a young child, she ate in other people's homes, tried different brands of cereal, and helped prepare meals. You let her know that you ate spaghetti sauce just like this when you were little, and gave her an "in" to her own family traditions by telling her why your family eats this way. Eventually she tried foods from other cultures and traditions. Maybe she visited a farm or orchard. Maybe she shopped in a bakery with you and noted all the different shapes and sorts of bread. She asked questions. And she sorted things out in her own mind: She discovered that she likes bagels but not hard rolls, rye without caraway, whole wheat rather than pumpernickel. She understood the reason for slicing bread, but wasn't sure why some loaves should be braided and not others. Bread, like cars and coats and shoes and dogs, helped your child to see the different needs, interests, passions of different people. It served as a window through which she could connect with others.

Sure, you could have taught her—and still could teach her—a minicourse on food, with lessons on cultures, traditions, nutritional value, and production processes. After all, that's how so many things are learned, aren't they—from the top down? How much better to learn from the bottom up, not just about food, but about anything she experiences daily: getting along with others, solving problems on her own and in a group, finding out how people express themselves, understanding different cultures in geography, history, and the community.

Young children learn best through concrete, physical, sensorial experiences and explorations of situations, stories, ideas, and problems before moving on to global explanations and analyses. We—parents and teachers—need to help children "do" social studies from the bottom up.

So, how do you get your child involved in exploring history, asking questions about his neighborhood, considering why you eat what you eat and why you wear what you wear, wondering about other languages, hearing the messages in music, seeing the daydreams and the reality inside a painting. He already is. A baby begins observing as soon as he is born, reaches out a hand, studies a smiling face. A child begins to file away specifics, later using them to make categories, explanations, and judgments. For example, he sorts familiar voices from strange voices, prefers rhyming poems to regular conversation, begins to understand the differences between anger, joy, and sadness. He grows to understand that so many things around him can be grouped in certain ways: feet and skateboards and chariots and wheelchairs and Ferraris and covered wagons and helicopters are all means by which people have gotten from here to there; trees and caves and blanket forts and apartment towers and motor homes and Greek Revival houses and sod houses and ancient Irish beehive huts are all ways people have had shelter from the elements. Involved with so many, many sights and sounds and events and experiences, your child will naturally develop his own understanding of categories, relationships, interactions, and connections.

Just as your child learns to ask for food that pleases her the most, she learns to ask questions that lead to stories, to information, to responses and reactions, and to new questions. This book offers you the information you need to help your child find out what she wants to know and to increase her explorations through every available avenue. You'll find ways to support your child as she moves from observing and interacting with the people near her to exploring more purposefully her interest in the workings of the larger world of neighborhood, school, community, nation, and globe. You'll help her take the step from asking "Why do you . . ." to posing questions that start "What would happen if . . ." and have answers that start "Maybe this is how it is . . . ."

Note that many of the activities in this book overlap with other subject areas. Clearly a child who talks about a relationship between two entities—a mother and a child, a person and a building, a city and a river—is learning the language to talk, read, and write about social studies situations. But a child who comes to understand that farmers may make use of a fertile river valley despite the threat of flood learns social studies as well as science, economics, and agriculture. And a child who echoes a Cab Calloway chant, listens to a rap song, or hears a story sung operatically gathers information about rhythm and patterns, key concepts of both arts and math.

Understanding Processes

In most learning, there's a natural progression. In swimming, a child goes from dabbling and splashing to wading and blowing bubbles, and then eventually from rudimentary strokes to surface dives. In math, a child goes from reciting numerals to actually counting—matching a numeral to an object. With social studies, too, there's a progression, a process that a child goes through in order to grasp key concepts.

The concept of time, for example, is one of the trickiest concepts for any person to understand, and one which remains, through life, largely subjective.

A friend of mine recalls as a child having vivid, confused pictures of the past. The past was biblical times, for her. And it was also colonial times. At six, she wondered which was the real past, and came quite slowly to the realization that they were both past, in different points on the timeline of life.

Points in time and space—stories and places—swirl around a young child's mind until she builds some frames of reference, some hooks in history and geography on which to hang new information.

For babies, the only real point in time is *now.* As they grow, they begin to comprehend *today.* Young children get *yesterday, today,* and *tomorrow,* but nothing much beyond. Eventually, their understanding broadens to include ideas like *this weekend, last summer, on your birthday, soon, later,* and *used to be.* Time as a measurement, broken down into minutes, hours, days, and weeks, is an incredibly hard concept to grasp, one that most children don't truly understand (regardless of whether they've learned to tell time) until ten or twelve years of age.

How does a child build a concept of the timeline of life? By understanding the timeline of his own life. One afternoon his father tells him, "After you get up from your nap, we'll go to the playground. Then we'll get food for dinner and come home and cook." The child begins to figure out that things happen in progression, in a sequence over time.

Kids need to figure out for themselves what it all means, to make their own meaning of the swirl of events and stories and ideas that they hear and read about. They need to be encouraged to create their own time framework, their own understanding of cultures and happenings and people, their own interpretation of *first, next, then, eventually.* They need first to understand how time progresses in their own daily routines—little schedules of events—and then expand that awareness to grasp the concepts of *years, centuries, ages.*

In order for you as a parent to understand and appreciate your child's ability to make connections with other people, places, and times, it helps to understand the process she goes through to reach those goals. It helps your child to be able to see the process too. The first thing she needs to do with any idea is to explore it, experience it, discuss it. There is a natural progression from watching and touching, to asking "Can I try?" "Who gets to go first?" "What do you think is going to happen next?" "When did people start giving babies bottles?" to getting answers to questions by projecting possibilities and researching, to using the bare bones of an event to create a story that makes sense to her.

Skills and Concepts

While most of the educational material on the market focuses on building specific skills and instilling specific information, this book will help your child develop an understanding of needed concepts.

A *skill* is an activity that can be learned and that can improve with practice; for example, cutting with scissors, riding a tricycle, or identifying states by their shapes. A *concept,* on the other hand, is something that can't be taught directly. It's something each and every person comes to understand on his or her own. An example of a key concept in social studies is the idea that a piece of land can be represented on a map. A child may think that a map is just a pretty pattern, that it fits together because it is a jigsaw puzzle, that the border between New York and New Jersey can only be a river, never a line. Maps are a tough concept. Who would have thought that the enormous earth could be compacted into a globe the size of a basketball? How could that enormous state of Connecticut, which takes four whole hours to drive through (at highway speeds), show up as a teensy puzzle piece the size of somebody's baby tooth?

Eventually, your child's incredulity gives way to an understanding that large physical objects can indeed be represented in pastel colors on paper. Sure, you can sit him down with your atlas and quiz him on the borders of Kentucky, instruct him on north, south, east, and west, and even encourage him to follow the route your car takes. Still, your child's true grasp of maps relies on his ability to note that when he draws someone on a piece of paper, the person isn't as big on paper as in real life. It helps if he's had some experience in drawing a picture of a small familiar area—a room, a block, a town—and then labeled it with names of businesses, friends' houses, streets, and other landmarks. The acquisition of a concept happens over time. It fades in and out, and takes hold only after much experience. People who are enthusiastic about maps are generally those who are able to use their imaginations to "see" what the map represents—to compare it to what they already know and to envision new and amazing lands. By seeing maps in close association with real places, your child will grasp the concept because of his experiences. He'll realize that maps stand for areas where people live, where they have homes.

He'll absorb other concepts too: scale, size, distance, and the relationship between cultures and geography.

This is not to say that children don't acquire skills through activities. For example, Activity 4: Sign Me Up involves working with your child to develop hand signals based on or similar to American Sign Language. Yes, your child will learn some signs, but even more, she'll realize that there are different ways of expressing similar ideas. She'll gain a respect for other languages and develop a positive curiosity for the ways people communicate. Sure, it might seem faster just to switch on a foreign-language cable station and say, "Hey, listen!" But would it be the same? Would your child understand the language as personally, as gradually, as enjoyably? Would there be room for trial and error, searching and finding, nonsense and reality, you and me? How much more valuable it is to get your child inside a new language, to encourage her to create her own expressions, and to share them together.

Every experience provided through the activities in this book will help your child to develop concepts that will lead to a deeper understanding of the world, an appreciation of past and present, and respect for the people who live and create in it.

About the Activities

The activities in this book are chock-full of my philosophy of learning. They will help you create cultural learning experiences out of just about any situation, in and out of your home. They encompass games, chores, work, and play. The activities are organized into the following areas:

Part One:	**Understanding People.** These activities help your child to understand the common basic needs of people for food, clothing, shelter, self-expression, and interaction.
Part Two:	**We're in This Together.** These activities feature strategies and games for understanding and getting along with others.
Part Three:	**A Whole World Out There.** Through these activities, you and your child explore stories of time and space and the concepts behind them.

Part Four: **Eyes, Ears, Body, and Soul.** Music, art, and drama are the focus of these activities.

You don't have to pursue the activities in order. Jump around. Pick and choose. Generally, it's best to choose what appeals to you and to your child's interests, doing activities from each section, picking out what fits in with things you do already, and most of all, letting activities arise from your child's questions and interests. Change, adapt, and mold the activity to make it your own.

For each activity, you'll see the following structure:

- **Name of Activity:** the title, followed by a few words about the heart of the activity
- **Helps Develop:** concepts and skills addressed
- **You'll Need:** a list of materials
- **Before You Begin:** actions to take and things to consider before starting
- **What to Do:** step-by-step directions
- **Follow-up Activities:** ways to redo and build on the activity in the future
- **What's Happening:** an explanation of what your child stands to gain from the activity
- **Moving Ahead:** ways to take the activity to a higher level
- **Helpful Hint:** a word of advice or a reference to a helpful book or material

Each activity is labeled with the places you're most likely to use it: around the house, out and about (market, mall, library, pool), close to home (backyard, garden, park, street, woods), and from here to there (in transit, public or private).

How You Can Get the Most Out of the Activities
Understand Your Child's Development

"She knows the names of all fifty states."

"He's such a jazz buff."

"My child wants to know about everything that comes on the news."

There's a popular notion in this country that every parent

dreams his or her child could grow up to become president. To hear parents tell it, each child is uniquely qualified. But a brief look at the diverse ages of the U.S. presidents at election time reveals that different people develop different abilities at different ages and, regardless of appearances, not everyone meets challenges in the same way. To be president, one needs a command of politics and history, as well as the ability to communicate clearly, get along with people, and maintain a certain public persona. To put it mildly, these are attributes that worry a lot of parents (not to mention the rest of the electorate).

It's easy to want your child to leap ahead to a clear understanding of the forces that shape today's world. And all of us want our children to be liked, a trait that translates into getting along with others. The fact remains that these are some of the most difficult capabilities in the world to grasp firmly. These capabilities depend on experience, perception, sensitivity, and confidence, all of which take time to develop.

Just as kids develop at different rates physically—look at all the shapes and sizes of your child's playmates—their rates of emotional, social, and intellectual development are likewise diverse. Celebrate how interesting your child's development is rather than worry about it. "How?" you ask. Here are a few basic tips:

- **Don't push.** When your child comes home from a day of negotiations at school or child care and wants to crawl into your lap, let him. Accept that he's been stretching himself, and that now he needs to bounce back a little. Don't see it as a regression. As a rule, hug your kid until *he* moves away.

- **Don't compare.** "Comparisons are odious," said a poet. They are not needed in formal education, and certainly not in the kind of informal education that is the premise of this book. This is especially important when you have more than one child. Encourage each child to respect the other's way of looking at things, and you've done the community —and society—a favor.

- **Don't have an agenda.** The writers of materials on the market today that make your child a "real" preschooler, kindergartner, first grader, or whatever are entitled to their opinions. I submit that if your child is encouraged to fully experience her daily life, to explore the meanings in everyday events and objects, and to follow the interests she's passionate about, she'll be much better prepared than a child who's been coached and quizzed on arbitrary knowledge without the necessary scaffolding of concepts and skills. Let your child's questions frame her learning.

Accept Your Child's Questions

There is one golden rule of education: *Every question is a good question.* This can be harder to deal with than you think. You may be called on to help your child find answers to questions such as "How did people go to the bathroom in Cleopatra's time?" or "Why didn't Benjamin Franklin get electrocuted?" The best thing you can do is simply answer, "That's a good question. I wonder how we can find out." Then set about—with your child—looking for the answer. As you do, model for your child how to ask librarians, museum staff, or other experts for help. Don't be afraid to look like you don't know what you're doing. Your child doesn't know either. After following you around for a couple of years, giving you ideas and working with you, he'll be doing research on his own. And he'll have learned an invaluable lesson: he won't be afraid of not knowing.

Accepting all questions can be tough when they deal with touchy issues such as death, war, crime, or reproduction. How well I remember being told as a child, "You don't need to know that now. You'll find out when you're older." I thought that I'd grow up and one day just *know* those things. Meanwhile, I had my own ideas and theories and fears, right or wrong ones, that never got out in the open because they were shut down.

My advice is, when you get a tough question, turn it around. Ask your child what she thinks. Your child is asking the question because of something interesting that she's heard or seen. During the Persian Gulf War, a few children in my school began talking about the war. When they asked a teacher about war, she turned the question around: "Well, what do *you* think war is?" One answered, "It's when one person throws a rock at another." He'd heard *Iraq* as *a rock*.

Be careful also not to give excessive information. Describe something basically, without great detail, filling in specifics if your child presses you. He'll let you know when his curiosity has been satisfied, and you'll show your respect and faith in his ability to understand by not giving him the brush-off.

Give Your Child Historical Hooks

I'll never forget my father's story of going to visit a fire station at age twelve. He was invited to sit atop the fire horse, a huge variety of workhorse no longer seen today. His recollection, made so alive for me, was that the horse's back was so broad he couldn't get his legs around it.

That story gave me insight into what my father was like at age twelve. Just as important, throughout my life, it has given me a hook—an image, a story, an experience—on which to hang hats full of historical facts and features. When I think of that time period, it helps me to realize that fire engines were drawn by horses, that boys wore knickers, that workhorses were gigantic and vitally important to the community.

A five-year-old named Emily has a big sister who reads her stories from the American Girls series as well as the Little House books by Laura Ingalls Wilder. Those books are Emily's history hooks. On Presidents' Day, when she heard a story about George Washington, she came home and asked her mother, "Was George Washington in Laura's time? In Samantha's time? Oh! In Felicity's time!" Yes, Felicity's time, when the colonies were getting ready for the Revolution, when little girls wore shoes that fit equally well on either foot, when they took dancing lessons to learn the minuet. For Emily, the stories about those girls—some real, some made to seem real—are hooks for the kind of history she'll learn in school.

Read your child these kinds of story, and as he learns more history, looks at artwork, hears music, or watches dance, he'll fit these experiences into his framework of learning. Talk about what things were like in past time. What did people eat? Where did they sleep? Were there people then? He'll get hooked into time periods, and as he learns about new events, he'll want to fit them into what he already knows. Were there dinosaurs in America when the Pilgrims came?

Extend Your Child's Imagination to Other Cultures, Times, and Places

Start in your own backyard, figuratively and literally. A friend's daughter was dangling upside down by her knees from an ancient apple tree in her yard. She dropped to the ground, and beside her hand she found a ring—a child's ring that just fit her finger. "I wonder . . ." said her father. Together, they concocted a story about the child who had lived there years before, when the tree was first planted, who lost her ring while hanging upside down. They visited the local library and found a lithograph of their town, a sort of aerial view which showed that an apple orchard had thrived there long before the house was built. Thus, the girl who lost the ring was a farmer's daughter. The questions came thick and fast: Where did she go to school? How long would she have gone? What kind of chores did she have to do? And, inevitably, was there a bathroom in her house? What did she wear, besides the ring?

Look at the history lesson this child got. History happens, and most of it isn't documented. People's lives were different and changed slowly, leaving behind only clues. History is a story. History is a mystery. And, as with everything else, there are no right answers.

It helps your young child to learn all he can about what makes other people alike, as well as what makes them unique. The best thing that you can do to facilitate this learning is to discourage your child from making judgments and to watch your own words and actions. When your child tries a new food or sees a new kind of clothing or hears a new dialect, encourage him to describe and think of these things as new, interesting, or different, rather than weird or strange.

Give Your Child Strategies for Dealing with Others

"Just Say No" is a great idea in theory, but in practice children need experience with several different strategies for dealing with others, for stating their positions loud and clear, and for making their needs known in a polite way.

- *Shake hands.* One of the simplest things I teach children to do is to shake hands with people they meet. It's an effective way for children to learn one of their culture's customs, to greet anyone of any age, to cope with shyness, and to waylay overly affectionate adults.

- *Cooperate.* Another thing I strongly believe in is: You don't have to share. Perhaps that idea seems wrong in a book that has a goal of helping children to cooperate and communicate with others. But think about what it means. A child who takes a toy or project from a shelf takes it out of the public domain. After that, anyone who wants to play with her or with it asks permission: "Can I work (or play) with you?" Possible responses must all be polite:

"No, but thank you for offering. I want to do this myself today."

"Sure. Why don't you do the . . ."

"No, but if you want I'll eat lunch with you later."

True cooperation means coming to agreement on what needs to be done and on who will do what. If kids know that they're free to express their own interests and preferences, there's less fear and more confidence. You can introduce this kind of communication in your home, refusing help when you don't want it, negotiating tasks or a specific part of a task, and enabling your child to do the same when she's the one doing a job.

- *Mediate.* Likewise, two children who disagree can be invited to do a number of things. They can:

  Be encouraged to find a solution together, rather than have a solution imposed on them.

  Ask someone else to be a mediator. A mediator hears both sides, then offers a solution or encourages the people involved to find a solution together.

  Play Slap Hands (see Activity 28).

Getting Your Child Started with Social Studies and the Arts

So you want to get your child started? If he is already born, then you *have* already started, through the atmosphere you've created in your home. When children are involved in building, sorting, caring for others (including pets) and being cared for themselves, helping with shopping, cooking, eating, playing with friends or brothers and sisters or parents, hearing stories, watching television, checking out old photo albums, going to religious services, going to parades, taking karate or gymnastics or violin lessons, painting, drawing, or making mud pies, and doing other real-life cultural activities, they learn to do history, civics, geography, and the arts as a natural part of life. Families foster this learning at home by gathering an assortment of interesting goods, encouraging experimentation and discussion, setting up many interesting situations, playing games, and suggesting activities at appropriate times. The atmosphere in these homes is what I call a cultural connections stew. The best stews are the ones that take a long time, that start in the morning with a bone and some water and simmer all day, with new ingredients added as the day goes by: herbs, wine, vegetables. What I wish for all children is that they might grow up sloshing around in a cultural stew in their homes.

You can create a cultural stew for your child out of all the objects—things you might not typically think of as social studies or art materials—around the house and the backyard. Here are just a few of the "ingredients" she will benefit from: food, gardens, flowers, building blocks, modeling clay, paper, pencils, paint, fabric, old clothes, photo albums, baby books, letters, newspapers, the television set, electricity, appliances, the telephone book, the walls, the floor, the radiator. Then there is everything that comes into the house that involves people, new ideas, other places, food, housing, transportation, traditions, customs, and *change*.

There's another vital ingredient, and it's free: talk. One of the most important things you can do as a fellow historian or student of culture is to model your thought processes. Share your questions with your child, speak aloud as you wonder about something, be slow to provide definitive answers and quick to encourage him to think and draw his own conclusions. Voice your concerns as open-ended questions ("I wonder what would happen if you didn't get a vaccination?"), explore unfamiliar areas with your child (rather than limit him to your experience), let him challenge your ideas, and let him catch you being wrong. It's important for your child to know that mistakes are part of learning.

Make stories of all kinds available to your child in the form of books, magazines, and newspapers. Use photographs and past experiences and postcards and maps to create stories based on your own life and the lives of family and friends. Create fantasies about life on other planets, about fairies in the backyard, about travel to other places. Encourage your child to solve problems around the house through her own inventions and innovations. Pose family questions to the group in general, brainstorm solutions, and take a vote on the matter at hand.

Visit museums and talk to the people who work there. Discuss what you hear on the news, read on signs, or see in the street. Learn about places you visit by reading stories about their history, finding out all you can about the people who live there now, studying maps and walking around, listening with open ears as well as an open mind.

Together with your child, create traditions for celebrations, daily events, and difficult times (such as dentist visits). Help him to see that traditions started with people like you who figured out interesting ways to do things.

Above all, nurture an atmosphere of acceptance of religions, cultures, races, and ideologies while helping your child to understand your own. I believe that in society there is nothing more valuable than respect, collaboration, and flexibility in problem solving. If your child learns these things at a young age, she will have a far greater advantage than the child who is merely well-informed.

Jumping-Off Point

The first historian was the first person who told a story based on something he or she had done or seen. Early artists and musicians, too, made their own sense of the world and interpreted it for others. Listen to your child as he describes a drawing or a scenario he's set up with dolls or toys.

> "This is a ladybug, and she's flying over our house to look down the chimney and see if there's any fire coming out."

> "This is a war. These two guys are going to blow up this tunnel. Then people will have to use the bridge."

> "Snow White's in the woods looking for bad mushrooms to feed the wicked queen."

Any artwork, any piece of music, any story is a connection, a representation of life as important as any relic archaeologists have dug up—and maybe more important because it provides a look into a person's mind and heart, rather than just a look at an item he or she touched. Encourage your child to tell stories about things she sees: "What would it have been like to meet that dinosaur?" "Can you imagine walking into a cave and seeing paintings that no one has looked at for thousands and thousands of years?" "What would it be like to live on an island in the ocean?" The best historians, anthropologists, and archaeologists are not just those who are good at finding things—although surely research skills and plain old serendipity play a part. No, the champs are those who can use their imaginations, their frames of reference, and the facts at hand to create a story that makes sense to people today.

History, like science, is always changing. Today's most widely accepted story is yesterday's cutting-edge proclamation and tomorrow's outmoded theory. During your child's school life, textbooks will continue to change radically as notions of political correctness and historical truth change with the wind. Encourage your child to be open and flexible, to make history truly part of *his* (or *her*) *story*, to accept many ideas, exploring them, playing with them, and sifting through them for what is most meaningful both to your child and to the others on this planet.

PART ONE

Understanding People

History is about people: what they do, how they live, how they clothe, shelter, feed, and express themselves. The study of history invites comparisons between past and present, then and now. And to make comparisons, you need commonalties. That's what this section is all about. For your child, history means first recognizing what makes people people—and then going on to find out how people change.

There's geography here too. The word geography literally means "stories about land." You can't have stories without people, and you don't have people without stories. Through these activities, you and your child can explore your own land and use your imagination —and some great ideas from this book —to travel to other lands.

1 The Grandparents of Pajamas

Helps develop: cross-cultural commonalities, problem-solving skills, understanding of relationship between time and history

"What were the grandparents of pajamas?" a child asked me. In other words, what did people wear to bed in the good old days?

You'll Need library, museum, or historical society

Before You Begin Encourage your child to think about the past. The subject may be pajamas, or it may be toilets, lunch, flashlights, underwear, dolls, beds—anything that interests a child enough to make him ask, "Did you have a toilet in your house when you were little?" or "Did George Washington wear pajamas?"

What to Do

1 When your child asks a question about the past, start with a response from your own history. "Well, I know things have changed. We didn't have Power Rangers pajamas . . . . Fabrics are fire-resistant now. . . . I wore a nightgown. . . ."

2 Move farther back in time. Ask someone older than you what sleepwear he or she wore in childhood.

3 Say to your child, "I wonder how we could find out what people wore before that . . . in George Washington's time . . . even earlier."

4 Go to the library or to a museum or historical society. With your child, ask the librarian or curator to help you find the answer to your question.

Follow-up Activity Fascinating answers lead to more questions. The pajama question, for example, may lead to a discussion of colonial farmers' long underwear (over which many threw their minuteman uniforms). If you search farther back, you may discover that some medieval peasants in Europe didn't wear pajamas at all; the peasants were sewn into their clothes in autumn and wore the same outfit until spring.

Children are deeply involved in the details of daily life and basic bodily functions: cooking, eating, washing, getting sick, going to the bathroom, sleeping. And rightly so. They are figuring out how these things are done today. History becomes most real to children when it is presented in everyday terms. Through this activity, you help your child to see that people did the same things, but somewhat differently, a long time ago and in different places. Children are acting like historians as they piece together the past from what's available in the present.

When you take your child to a library, museum, or historical society and consult an expert or a reference librarian, you model how people find out information they want to know about the past. Research is a key process that can't be begun too soon in a child's life.

Moving Ahead Visiting museums gives children moving experiences of how people lived in earlier times. Hands-on museums are great, but you can turn even a stodgy glasscase exhibit into an interactive experience by talking to your child about it and helping him to see what it shows about the way life used to be. Talk about how the objects might have looked when new, how the child felt who wore the dress, what the view outside the house was like, how it felt to empty the chamber pot in the morning.

Helpful Hint Ask your librarian to help you find old copies of Sears or Montgomery Ward mail-order catalogs, which much of America relied on for clothing. Such catalogs are a rich resource in terms of the fashions people wore. Your child will be fascinated by the items, and you'll be amazed by the prices.

2 Wrappers!

How many ways can you wear a piece of fabric?

You'll Need several lengths of fabric 2 to 3 yards (2 to 3 m) long and of various widths (sheets and towels work great!); drawing paper and pencils *or* camera

Before You Begin Talk with your child about the basic needs of life: food, shelter, clothing.

What to Do
1 Give your child a length of fabric and take one for yourself.
2 Wonder aloud, "Could a person wear this as clothing? How?"
3 Encourage your child to try wrapping her cloth around her body. Wrap your cloth however you please.
4 Talk about what areas of the body are essential to cover. Would your outfits be suitable in any weather? What else could be added?

Follow-up Activities
- Experiment with many different clothing configurations. Come up with an assortment of outfits.
- Keep track of your outfit designs by drawing them or taking pictures.
- Talk about various ways that the outfits could be finished and secured. Is it necessary to have sleeves, pants legs, buttons, zippers, underwear?

- Find out together about clothing technology. What did people do before zippers, snaps, and Velcro? Who invented these things?

What's Happening

Through this activity you're taking your child to the level of the first person who picked up an animal skin or a leaf and used it as a body covering. You're also opening your child's mind to understand the purpose and construction of clothing, the essentials and the nonessentials. Focus here and now on encouraging your child to see alternatives as different, *not strange*. When your child sees clothing from other cultures, she'll remember this experience and note with interest the ways that people solve the clothing problem.

Moving Ahead

Be on the lookout on television, in books or magazines, and on the street for people wearing different kinds of clothing. Note all the different kinds of coats. Look for skirts, ponchos, saris, togas, and other apparel made with just one piece of cloth. Examine, also, your child's own clothes. How many different pieces of fabric are they made of? How are the pieces put together?

Helpful Hint

Encourage your child to make clothes for dolls, stuffed animals, herself. You don't need patterns or a sewing machine, just needle and thread, a pair of scissors, and a piece of fabric. Throw out preconceived notions of what a shirt or a pair of pants should be, and guide your child to create her own garments.

3 Every Picture Tells a Story

Every picture is worth a thousand words.
So get it in writing.

Helps develop:
sense of history as the story of life, empathy for others, understanding of time as a sequence of events

You'll Need   current family photo album; pen and labels *or* special pen for writing on paper or acetate album pages; photo album from your past; paper and pencil *or* tape recorder

Before You Begin   Go through your photo album with your child. Ask if your child's grandchild will know the stories behind the pictures.

What to Do   **1** Ask your child to help you recall one of the events pictured in your album.

2 Talk about the event with your child. Discuss what he remembers, and tell him what you remember. Consider the point of view of someone who wasn't there. What would that person need to know?

3 Together, write a caption for the photograph.

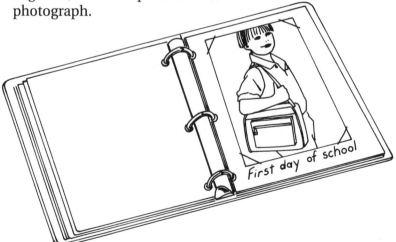

First day of school

Follow-up Activities
- Go through an album from your past with your child. Tell him the stories behind the pictures. Ask him to help you write captions so that his grandchildren will know about you and your life through the pictures.
- Write or tape-record the stories of the photos.
- See if you can find pictures in the current album that are similar in "feel" to the past photos.

What's Happening   Anytime that you and your child look at a photo album, you help him to gain an understanding of the passage of time and to build ideas about memory. Memory is a funny thing. It involves point of view, values, and judgments, and it changes over time. Your child may be interested to realize that you remember things pictured in your albums differently from him, or that you can tell stories about things he did that he can't recall. Through this activity you look into the past and speculate about—and plan for—the future.

Moving Ahead   Plan a small album—a photo essay, really—about your child's day. Encourage him to plan it with you, set up and pose for the photographs, edit and select photographs, make the album, and write the captions.

Helpful Hint   Through baby books and other scrapbooks, your child realizes that objects hold stories too. Such an understanding will help him imagine stories when he looks at museum pieces—and other old things—that reflect people's lives.

4 Sign Me Up

H*elps develop: understanding of language, gesture, and symbolism; concept of communication as a basic human need*

"I love you." Besides using words, how many ways do people communicate that idea?

You'll Need you and your child

Before You Begin Discuss with your child that gestures stand for ideas and that feelings can be read through body language.

What to Do

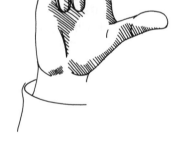

1 Catch your child using a hand or head gesture: nodding her head, holding up a finger to say *wait* or *come here*, waving *hello* or *good-bye*.

2 Ask, "What are you saying when you do that?" Encourage her to put her gesture into spoken words.

3 Share some examples of sign language with your child
- The American Sign Language sign for "I love you": fist with thumb, index finger, and pinkie raised, as shown in the illustration
- The "A-OK" sign: circle made with thumb and index finger, other three fingers raised
- The peace or victory sign: index and middle fingers raised in a V, thumb over other two fingers

4 Encourage your child to think up a sign of her own and tell you what it means.

Follow-up Activities Here are some other ways to explore signs and symbols:
- Wonder together about the meaning of traffic-sign symbols.
- Check signs and storefronts for logos and symbols that represent different businesses (the golden arches, the big yellow seashell, logos on soft drink bottles, etc.).

- Develop secret signals to use in company—something that your child can use to tell you she wants to go home, that she's happy and fine, and so forth.
- Develop signals to use together. One father has a special signal he uses with his daughter to indicate that no matter what she tells him, he promises to respond calmly. (They originated the signal when she was three and wanted to tell him amazing secrets; it's still in play now that she's in her teens.)

What's Happening *Every culture needs to communicate; every person needs to express himself or herself. Through this activity, you show your child that there are many ways to get an idea or feeling across. Use it as a lead-in to foreign languages, once again stressing that* different *doesn't mean* weird.

Moving Ahead Explore rebuses (pictures that stand for words or syllables) with your child, then move into other kinds of codes that involve symbols for letters or words.

Helpful Hint Try these books:
- *Handtalk: An ABC of Finger Spelling and Sign Language* by Remy Charlip and Mary B. Miller (Macmillan, 1987)
- *Handtalk School* by Mary Beth Miller and George Ancona (Macmillan, 1991)

5 Our Town

Helps develop: *community feeling, concept of interrelatedness of people in a community, beginning understanding of what people do and need to do for a town to function*

What's doing in your town?

You'll Need camera (optional); paper, pencils, crayons or markers, and other bookmaking materials

Before You Begin Talk with your child about your neighborhood and town. Discuss the different things that go on where you live, and the many interesting people who live there.

What to Do

1 Take a walk through your neighborhood or town. You can do this as part of an errand-running day, but better yet, make the purpose of the walk to notice things, to look around, to explore. If you like, take your camera along and snap photos.

2 Back home, invite your child to recall with you the sights and sounds you experienced together. Whom did you see or talk to? What buildings and businesses did you pass? What was going on in one place or another?

3 Invite your child to make a book about your walk through town. Together, choose highlights to include in your book. If you took photographs, let your child select a few. Ask your child to draw pictures, and help him write captions for them.

Follow-up Activities

• Encourage your child to share his book with family members and friends. Discuss with other people what their favorite parts of town are and what they know about the people who live and work there.

- Suggest that your child share his book with town officials, with a local newspaper, or with the children's librarian. Each of these sources may give you information about the places you pictured or wrote about with your child, and talking to them will help your child to understand the importance to different people of certain parts of your town or neighborhood.

What's Happening *First and foremost, you and your child are sharing your impressions about a place that you rely on for business, groceries, postal services, and a multitude of other things. By talking about each building, business, and person, you help your child to see the many roles a town plays in people's lives. What's more, you focus his attention on places and his passage through them, helping him to see that events happen in sequence and that a physical place can be represented on paper. This provides important support for developing concepts of time and space.*

Moving Ahead Travel around. Compare your neighborhood or town to others. Check out different malls. Help your child to see that every community needs people and places to fill important roles. Encourage your child to see the communities' commonalities and to appreciate their differences. Follow your child's specific interest. One child I know became a garbage truck maven, conversant with the different types of trucks, recycling vehicles, and garbage removal systems. He was able to relate trucks to different dumping areas and systems, and to understand different communities through his interest.

Helpful Hint Nonfiction books on various topics can be used to help your child focus on town facilities and to see them in general terms as compared to facilities in other towns. Try these:
- *The Best Town in the World* by Byrd Baylor (Macmillan, 1983)
- *Sing a Song of People* by Lois Lenski (Little, Brown, 1987)
- *Delivery Van: Words for Town and Country* by Betsy Maestro (Houghton Mifflin, 1990)

6 You're a Card

Helps develop: ability to categorize according to common characteristics, ability to make generalizations

*What do you have in common with a pig?
With someone living in China?
With the moon?*

You'll Need   photographs, old magazines, and postcards; scissors; glue stick; 4-by-6-inch (10-by-15-cm) index cards; pencil

Before You Begin   Collect photographs of friends, family, animals, and places. Gather only those you won't mind using to make picture cards.

What to Do

1 Use your photographs, magazine cutouts, and postcards to create a set of cards. Glue the pictures on index cards and label with one or two words (mother pig, Aunt Kim, pyramid, etc.).

2 Show the cards one by one to your child, and talk about the various pictures.

3 Ask your child to pick out two cards that have something the same about them. This can be anything from appearance to location to habits. Invite her to explain her choice.

4 Take your turn. Pick two cards that have something in common, and talk about what that factor is.

Follow-up Activities

- Add more cards and keep playing.
- Try dividing all the cards into groups according to one characteristic. Say your characteristic is that the subject swims. You could divide the cards into things that swim and things that don't swim.
- Pull out all the people cards. Invite your child to think of all the attributes that these people share.

What's Happening   The ability to group objects by their characteristics is key to social studies and cultural understanding. It's important for children to see what unites people, animals, buildings, and landscapes, as well as what distinguishes them. Have you ever heard someone say of a person who is intimidating, "He puts his pants on one leg at a time, just like the rest of us."? That's a statement that appeals to the basic humanity in everyone. If your child grows up understanding that people everywhere have much in common, you'll have given her a good foundation for dealing flexibly with the differences between us.

Moving Ahead   Use this activity to help your child see what people and animals have in common. Talk about how people and animals stay warm, find food and shelter, and live with others.

Helpful Hint   Store your cards in a big basket or see-through box. As with any toy, let your child explore the cards on her own. Get involved later, when she has begun to sort things out. Your first words should be words of observation: "Hmm. You've put the pig with the dog and the cow. I wonder why. . . ."

7 History Hooks

Helps develop: *understanding of history, flexibility in thinking, skills in comparison and contrast*

People make history. The more your child understands about a person's life, the more he'll understand about the history that surrounds that person.

You'll Need character to study; book about character's time period; library or museum (optional); model-making materials

Before You Begin Notice when your child shows interest in a person, whether the person is real or fictitious. It could be anyone from the artist who painted a favorite picture to the real Leonardo (da Vinci, not the Ninja Turtle) to a princess in a castle. Help that person become a history hook — someone who stands for a time or place in history and makes it personal to your child.

What to Do **1** Talk about a person your child is interested in. Wonder with your child what daily life was like for that person. If the person lived in a castle, ask, "I wonder how it really felt to live in a castle."

2 Find a book with an illustration of a castle or whatever kind of structure the person may have lived in. This could be a factual book or a fairy tale. Look at the picture with your child. Together, see what you can determine about the person's life from this picture.

3 At your child's level and following your child's interest, talk more about the person's life. "I wonder what they did about garbage in Princess Esmeralda's time." This innocent statement can lead to a discussion of automotive vehicles ("There were no garbage trucks in Princess Esmeralda's time"), servants ("Surely the Princess didn't take out her own garbage, so who did it for her?"), or types of garbage ("What kind of garbage might they have had back then anyway? No plastic . . . little glass . . . no need for recycling . . . paper was very hard to come by and was not used for wrappings . . . fabric wrappings were reusable . . . hmm . . .").

Follow-up Activities
- Visit a library or museum for specific information about the time period or person in question.
- Create a model of your person's home. Use the model to trigger discussions about plumbing, cooking, dress, heating, and so on.

What's Happening

By building a realistic picture of life around a character, you'll give your child a history course. A child who realizes that George Washington didn't watch TV in his youth realizes that TV hasn't been here forever, and that over time changes take place—the human race develops new technology, manners, art, music, and methods for answering basic needs.

A child who plays with a historical doll, reads historical books, and learns about people in history (or types of people, such as medieval princesses) soon learns to ask, "Was that before so-and-so's time?" The more people your child learns about, the more clear, complete, and personal her understanding of history will be—and the more flexible her thinking about and fascination with the future will be.

Moving Ahead

In your daily life, as you and your child talk about your day, refer to the historical characters—including family members—your child knows, and ask him to consider what their take on your present lifestyle would be. Wherever you are, talk about how that place might have changed. Whatever you're doing, consider together how that task might have been done in earlier times. "When Granny and Granddad were little, they couldn't come to the shore for the weekend. It would have taken them a day to travel here. They came for a month." Or "Do you know, in so-and-so's time, there were farms all around where Central Park is now? The real city was miles away."

Helpful Hint

Read as many books as you can about as many different people in history as you can, as well as people from different races, religions, and cultures. Try:
- *People* by Peter Spier (Doubleday, 1980)
- *All the Colors of the Earth* by Sheila Hamanaka (William Morrow, 1994)

8 Eat Your Way through Cultures

through Cultures

Helps develop: *understanding of cultures, steps in a process, flexibility in solving a problem*

How many different ways do you know to bake bread or prepare rice?

You'll Need cookbooks; ingredients and tools for making a staple food such as bread, rice, or potatoes; bakery (optional)

Before You Begin Serve your child food from other cultures regularly.

What to Do

1 Involve your child in planning a meal. Say, "I wonder what kind of bread [or rice, etc.] we should have."

2 Invite your child to describe different kinds of bread she's seen or eaten. Talk about the different tastes, textures, and shapes, and the different places the breads come from. Which is baked at home? In a small bakery? In a bread factory?

3 Check your cookbook to find more kinds of bread. Read about them with your child and share photographs or illustrations.

4 Choose one type of bread to have for dinner. Have your child help you make it or help you shop for it. Compare it with the other possible choices.

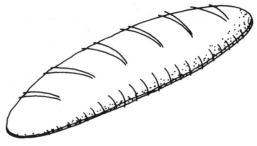

Follow-up Activities

- Try many different kinds of bread together. Talk about why people in different places make different kinds of bread.
- Make up your own kind of bread. Use a basic bread recipe from a cookbook, and invite your child to suggest ingredients to be added or to help you invent new shapes for the bread.
- Visit a bakery. Look at (and smell, if possible) the different kinds of bread.

What's Happening

Through this activity, you can not only explore together the cultural and personal reasons why you eat bread as you do, but also examine the ways that other people eat bread. You can expand your child's notion of what bread is—basically, a baked mixture of grains—and of the process by which bread is made. Most of all, through this activity your child develops an interest in and respect for other people's ways of doing things, and an understanding of where they—and she—fit in the world.

Moving Ahead

Try entire meals of foods from other cultures. This can be as simple as going to dinner at a friend's house or ordering Italian or Chinese take-away food for dinner.

Helpful Hint

Read:

- *How My Parents Learned to Eat* by Ina R. Friedman (Houghton Mifflin, 1984)
- *Too Many Tamales* by Gary Soto (Putnam, 1992)
- *Dumpling Soup* by Jama Kin Rattigan (Joy Street, 1992)

9 Where Did It Come From?

Helps develop: understanding of purpose and function of simple machines, understanding of process of developing a solution to a problem

Technology, *defined literally, means "the word of skill or art." Technology arises out of the problems that people have adapting to the world; it is the solutions they create to solve the problems.*

You'll Need simple machine (For the purpose of this activity, a machine can be anything from a zipper to a washing machine.); library or museum resources

Before You Begin Notice when your child is interested in a machine.

What to Do

1 When your child asks a question about a machine—how it works or why it's needed—answer with another question. "I wonder how we can find out?" or "What do you think?"

2 Talk with your child about the machine. Have him experiment with it and look at it closely. Show him what the buttons or other pieces do. With him, figure out the process by which the machine does its job.

3 Talk about the problem the machine solves. "Why do we need this thing? What would our lives be like if we didn't have it?"

4 Talk about what people did to solve the problem before the machine was invented.

Follow-up Activities
- Use library or museum resources to figure out earlier technology that was invented to solve the problem. For example, how did people keep their clothes closed before there were zippers? Before there were buttons?
- Find out together who invented the machine. What were the circumstances that led to the invention? Use library resources to find out about the inventor.

What's Happening

*C*hildren tend to understand the world as one magical phenomenon after another. This activity helps you guide your child to see that the things around him didn't just appear there. Each of them was made by someone, for a specific purpose, at a specific time. Each has evolved and will continue to evolve to become a better solution to the problem. By helping your child understand that inventions come as the result of people's efforts, you increase his understanding of how things change, and how people affect history.

Moving Ahead
Encourage your child to create an invention to solve a household problem. "I wonder how we can get a light in this bathroom where there's no plug." "The rabbit's water keeps freezing over." "What can we use to support these climbing morning-glory plants?" Through sewing, carpentry, and other fix-it skills, you can model the process of creating a technological solution.

Helpful Hints
- *Inventions and Discoveries* edited by Mark Young (Facts on File, 1993) contains some valuable information about inventions.
- *Steven Caney's Invention Book* by Steven Caney (Workman, 1985) describes some interesting projects to try with your child.
- You and your child can enjoy together *Samuel Todd's Book of Great Inventions,* a picture book by E. L. Konigsburg (Atheneum, 1991).

10 Write to Me, Baby

They say that with the dawn of fax communication, letter writing is back. What's cool about a fax is that it takes your handiwork exactly as is and sends it down the line.

You'll Need   paper and pencils; notebook (optional)

Before You Begin   Encourage your child to write even before she knows about spelling and grammar.

What to Do

1 Write your child a letter. Pass along some information, remind her of something, or just tell her she's a great kid. Add a little picture, if you want.

2 Tell your child you wrote her a letter. Then hand it over as a gift. Read it to her.

3 Make paper available so your child can write back to you. Encourage her to do so. Anything is acceptable—drawing, scribbles, invented spelling, or any other "writings"—as long as it encourages your child to communicate with you on paper.

4 Ask your child to read to you what she has written. Don't ever say, "I can't read this." Instead, say, "Would you read this to me?" If she protests that you have to read it, remind her that you read adult writing. Say simply, "I don't understand four-year-old writing."

5 Make it plain that you treasure your child's communication. Put it in a place where you keep or display precious things, and show her that you're putting it there.

Follow-up Activities
- Keep a family notebook on the kitchen counter or in an accessible drawer. Encourage all family members to write back and forth to each other. Use the notebook for ideas, lists, encouragement, reminders, or whatever you want. Again, accept all forms of communication.
- Encourage your child to write to other people. Mail or fax her communications. If you need to send a translation, say simply, "Grandpa doesn't know how to read four-year-old writing, so you tell me what it says, and I'll write it in forty-year-old writing for him."
- Share the mail with your child. Let her know what each piece is, read some mail aloud, and get her involved in sorting mail according to purpose or person.

What's Happening   Your child is getting firsthand experience with one of the chief ways that people express themselves and communicate with one another: through writing. It's vital that you encourage her to write fluidly at her own level, regardless of letterforms, construction, and spelling. As she grows and becomes a reader, these mechanical elements will settle into place.

Moving Ahead   Read plenty of books to your child. Also read signs as you drive along a road, flyers and brochures that you pick up in public places, and any other reading material you can get your eyes on. By doing this, you help your child to see all the different forms of communication that surround her and to understand the many voices of writers.

Helpful Hint   One of the other books in this series, *Ready, Set, Read and Write* (Wiley, 1995), is a great source of reading and writing activities. Check the bookstore or library where you found this book.

11 Make Your Own Desert, Swamp, Mountain...

What makes a desert a desert?

You'll Need different landscapes to look at; rectangular baking pan; modeling clay; sand; water; models of plants and animals; books about the landscape created

Before You Begin Point out different landscapes to your child—both in the natural world and in pictures.

What to Do
1 Talk with your child about a type of terrain that interests him. Encourage him to describe what he thinks the characteristics of the landscape are.

2 Say, "Would you like to make a small landscape?" Encourage your child to think up ways to make a small desert, swamp, or hill in a baking pan.

3 Make use of your child's ideas for materials, and/or suggest modeling clay, sand, and water. Talk about the makeup of this landscape with your child as he works. "I wonder why there's so much sand in the desert. Is there any water at all?"

4 As your child works, talk about the life that could exist in the place he's modeling. "I wonder what kind of plants grow in a swamp." "Water moccasins live here? What are they? What do they eat? Does anything eat them?"

5 Encourage your child to add models of plants and animals to his model. Talk about ways that people could exist in the landscape. "Could people live here? What kind of house would they have? What would they eat? How would they live?"

Follow-up Activities

- Find books and other information about the kind of landscape your child created.

- Explore with your child what might happen over time to the landscape. What would happen in winter? Would things change? Why or why not? What would happen if there were a storm? What sort of storm is it likely to have? When your child asks a question you can't answer, model how to find the answer.

What's Happening

A model is flexible: your child can explore what might happen if there were a flood, a freeze, or a drought, and project what the effect on the ecosystem might be. By creating a model of a landscape, your child explores the different characteristics of that landscape: The forces that make it what it is, the creatures and plants that live and grow there, and even how the particular landscape was originally formed. Through talking about a desert, for example, you can help your child understand how sand is made, that firm ground must be under the sand, that water sources still exist, and that deserts have a rich system of life—and that not all deserts have sand.

Moving Ahead

Visit a natural history museum to see how landscape models are created there. How do the models show what lives in each environment? How do they show how each living creature lives?

Helpful Hint

Books in Dorling Kindersley's Eyewitness Science series, such as *Desert, Pond,* and *Swamp,* are great resources.

12 Make Your Own Town

12 Make Your Own Town

Helps develop: *understanding of characteristics and workings of a town*

If I ruled the world . . .

You'll Need
different kinds of buildings to look at; wooden building blocks; dolls or other small figures; toy cars; small block (i.e., Lego) houses, animal figures, train set, etc. (optional)

Before You Begin
As you travel through your town and other towns with your child, point out the different kinds of buildings and talk about the purpose of each.

What to Do

1 Invite your child to help you build a town out of blocks.

2 Start by building something yourself that is easily recognizable to your child: the school, the library, your house, and the like.

3 Ask your child what she's going to build. Talk about the many features of a town. "What are some of the buildings in our town? Who lives here? How do people get around?" Guide your child to help build businesses, homes, transportation routes, parks, and other community necessities. Use dolls and toy cars, animal figures, and so forth.

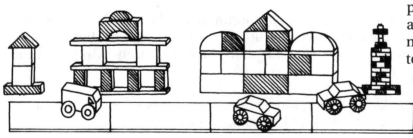

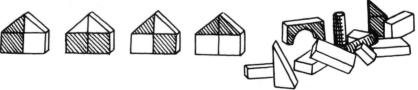

Follow-up Activities
- Give your town a name. Make building it a continuous process, to be added on to whenever your child gets a new idea.
- Choose one person who lives in the town. Take him (or her) through a day in the town. Where does he live? Where does he get food? Where does he walk his dog? Where does he go to school, buy clothes, keep his money, get medicine, and so forth?
- Add businesses and amusements that would make your town a better place—in your child's mind. Add people to visit those places and people to run them. Add houses for the people to live in.
- Name streets and businesses. As you do, wonder with your child how different spots in your town got their names.

What's Happening

By creating a model of your town, your child focuses attention on what goes into a town—what makes it a town where people live together, use each other's businesses, and plan for the future together. Through discussing the model, you can show your child how decisions she makes affect the life of the town.

Moving Ahead
- Time to take your block town down? Have your child draw it first, to help her remember it.
- Encourage your child to look down on the block town from above and draw a flat map of it. It may help to explore other maps as you do this, to give your child ideas and help her understand the concept.
- Design a futuristic town.
- Design a town as it might have been when Grandma was a baby.

Helpful Hint Read:
- *Town and Country* by Alice Provensen and Martin Provensen (Harcourt Brace, 1994)
- *Who Named My Street Magnolia?* by Sara Mark (Time-Life, 1995)

43

13 Make Your Own Celebration

It was going to be the hottest week of August. We were tired of the heat, tired of the backyard, tired of bugs. What else was there to do but throw a bug party? We dressed in bathing suits, made paper wings, walked barefoot through paint to make a caterpillar path on a large sheet of paper, and ate grasshopper pie (mint ice cream in a cookie crust with a plastic grasshopper on top). What a great new tradition for summer's dog days!

You'll Need materials determined by the celebration you and your child decide upon

Before You Begin As you experience family holidays with your child, discuss why you celebrate them as you do.

What to Do

1 Open the discussion by saying, "I wonder what we can celebrate today." If it's a popular holiday your family already celebrates, talk about the traditions that exist and how they came about. (Encourage your child to speculate, if you don't know.) Or you can make up a new, personal holiday with your child, and talk about how it might compare to other special days.

2 Brainstorm a list of ways to celebrate. These might include a parade, party, special meal or special food, songs, a dance, or even clothing—after all, we wear pajamas to a pajama party.

3 With your child, design a celebration plan. Say you choose a parade. Talk about what goes into a parade. What are your child's favorite aspects? What features could you replicate? What new ideas could you devise together? Encourage your child to be flexible. A full-size parade might not be practical. Instead, suggest a miniature parade with dolls and stuffed animals or toy vehicles.

4 Once you've planned your celebration, gather the materials you need. Shop for meal or recipe ingredients. Find what you need to make decorations or to spruce up your parade. Piece together costumes and try them on.

5 Stage your celebration. Invite others to take part, or use it as a special time between you and your child.

6 Celebrate!

Follow-up Activities
- Talk about how celebrations make people feel—about themselves, about each other, about the situation being celebrated.
- Mark your calendar for the next celebration. See Activity 41: Circular Calendar.

What's Happening

*D*oes "hands-on learning" apply to history? Sure it does, when you take a present-day event and make it into tomorrow's history. This activity helps children to see that history is something people make—that celebrations are something people just naturally like to do together, and that they can create their own. Traditions, holidays, and celebrations get demystified for kids who create their own, giving them more understanding—and curiosity—about the long-standing celebrations your family shares.

Moving Ahead
Walk through the calendar with your child to help him understand what's coming next. Your story of the year can include seasons, holidays, birthdays, and so on. It makes more sense to children than a discussion of days, weeks, and months—and it is personal to the events of each family.

Helpful Hint
Traditions don't have to be big things. They can be as simple as a game you play with your child when he's in the bathtub, as adult-friendly as a fancy dinner on Sunday nights, as everyday as renting a certain video on a certain day every year.

14 One Moment in Time

Helps develop: history hooks (see Activity 7: History Hooks); understanding of how things have changed in the world over time

Were there horses and buggies when you were little, Mom?

You'll Need   you and your child

Before You Begin   Talk with your child about other time periods—your childhood, your parents' childhoods, and so forth.

What to Do
1 Tell your child a story that begins "When I was little . . ." This can be an outgrowth of a question from your child, or just anything that pops into your head.

2 Add details to your story that show what times were like when you were young. Talk about the food you ate, the clothes you wore, what you and your friends or family did for fun, what school was like then.

3 Help your child to make comparisons between your childhood and her own. How were things different? How were they the same?

Follow-up Activities
• Tell the same story again on another day. (Kids love repetition.)

• Tell stories about yourself at different ages. Try to convey how you've changed over the years.

• Tell stories about your brothers and sisters and other people who are adults now and who are familiar to your child.

What's Happening

By telling your child a story from your childhood and embellishing it with details of setting, time, historical climate (Was there a lot of snow that year? Who was president?), you do several wonderful things. First, you bring your child into your personal life, your own history. Second, you let your child see that you were once a child like her; through your memories of childhood and your adult perspective on them, you can help your child see present-day situations in a new light. Third, you give your child a history hook—you. How many of us know certain years of this century as our parents' or grandparents' time? Through their eyes and their memories, our parents and grandparents have given us windows into history that are far different from the generalizations of history books. You can do the same with your child by telling her stories with an eye toward showing what life was like then.

Moving Ahead

Focus on anything or any area that interests your child (television? computers? candy?) and tell your child what that thing was like when you were young—or what life was like without it. Set the scene and tell a story that shows how you felt and thought about the thing in question.

Helpful Hint

Still got your old record collection? Get out your vinyl and spin records for your child. Talk about who's playing, what you were like when you got the records, how it felt to get a new record, and why you've kept them all these years.

15 Behind the Scenes

Helps develop: *understanding of processes and of businesses, understanding of people's roles in a community*

What in the world is more fascinating than other people and the things they make and do?

You'll Need   a business to study; library resources; paper, pencils, crayons or markers, and other bookmaking materials (optional); model-making materials or whatever materials are appropriate to imitate the business

Before You Begin   Find a business or enterprise that fascinates your child.

What to Do   **1** Ask your child a question about a business he's interested in. Focus on what happens behind the scenes or out of sight. "Where does the recycling truck go after it picks up our stuff?" "How do the bagels get made?" "How do these crayons get in this box and into the store?"

2 Ask your child to think with you of ways to find out what he wants to know. Could you ask the garbage collector or follow the truck to the dump? Visit the bagel shop? Get a book from the library about how crayons are made?

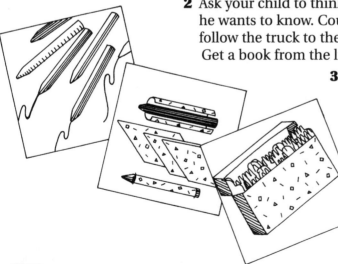

3 Choose one course of action and follow it with your child. Talk about what you see happening, and what it means.

4 Encourage your child to ask questions of the people available.

Follow-up Activities	• Talk about the people who work in the business. Consider how they learned to do what they do, how they feel about their work, and what they reveal about themselves through their activities.
	• Encourage your child to use paper and crayons or markers to make a book showing the process he's just learned about.
	• Encourage more questions about the business.
	• Encourage your child to build models of the recycling trucks, try making bagels at home, melt down crayons to see whether they look as they do in the crayon factory, and so forth. Taking action as a direct result of what has been learned is a great learning experience in itself.

What's Happening *Ask a young child what he or she wants to do for a living, and the child is most likely to mention something familiar: a firefighter (such clear-cut responsibilities!), a teacher, a parent, a Power Ranger. Give children more information about the businesses they interact with daily, and you help them to have a more complete image of their community—and a better understanding of work options that may be open to them. By talking to people and wangling invitations behind the scenes, you let your child see the processes—the step-by-step procedures over time—that make a product available, that make a business operative. You also model how to find needed information.*

Moving Ahead Ask your child if whether this business would have existed in Grandma's time . . . in Abraham Lincoln's time . . . in Cleopatra's time. If not, how did people get the job done?

Helpful Hints • Feed and nurture your child's passions. When artist Tomie de Paola was four years old, he drew and painted continually. His family invited a relative who was an artist to visit. He talked seriously to little Tomie about his job. As a result, Tomie announced that he wanted to be an artist. His parents set him up with the materials he needed to have his own small studio. Now a veteran illustrator, de Paola credits his parents with giving him the confidence—and the information—he needed to become the artist he was born to be.

- Try these great books about businesses—and about kids' curiosity about them:
  - *This Is a Great Place for a Hot Dog Stand* by Barney Saltzberg (Hyperion, 1995)
  - *Stop That Garbage Truck!* by Linda Glaser (Whitman, 1993)
  - *One Hundred Words about Working* by Richard Brown (Harcourt Brace, 1989)

16 Apples, Peaches, Pumpkin Pie

Eat in season, within reason.

You'll Need a food; the source of this food (field, orchard, lake, etc.); paper, pencils, and crayons

Before You Begin Show your child food growing on plants whenever you can. Let her see that tomatoes start small and green, and grow to be larger and red.

What to Do

1 Ask your child where she thinks a certain food comes from. Take her response seriously. "The refrigerator," "the store," "a farm," "a fishing boat" are all perfectly logical answers. If you're not sure where your child got her ideas, ask her, "Why do you think that?" Accept all responses.

2 Invite your child to help you trace the food back to its source. (It doesn't matter whether she got the answer "right"; the experience of this activity will add greatly to her understanding.

3 Take a step backward in the history of this food. Say it's an apple pie made with apples bought at a grocery store, shipped from an orchard, grown on a tree. Visit the produce manager at the grocery store. Find out how and where the apples were bagged, shipped, and delivered.

4 Keep backing up. Visit an orchard where apples are grown. Check out the trees. Talk about how people pick apples. If possible, pick some yourself. Ask an orchard employee how the trees are cared for, how long it takes an apple to grow, or any other questions that interest you or your child.

Follow-up Activities

- Encourage your child to document what she's found with a drawing or booklet about the food.
- Explore with your child how an apple pie is made or how other foods are prepared.
- Find out what's growing in your area now, in this season. Buy and eat some with your child.

What's Happening

In the old days, people ate only what was in season, and they lived—generally—much closer to the sources of food. Ask a city child today where milk comes from, and you'll get an interesting assortment of responses. Ask any child where chocolate comes from (or any adult, for that matter); the answer may surprise you. It helps children to understand where foods come from, how they're grown, and who and what is involved in getting them from the source to your dinner table. Such knowledge enables children to build a big picture of their world. This big picture will be an important asset for adults of the twenty-first century, who will have to work carefully to balance human needs with the needs of the environment that feeds them.

Moving Ahead

Grow your own food. Even apartment dwellers can plant a bean seed in a pot and watch it grow into food. If you've got the space to grow large plants, like pumpkins, do it.

Helpful Hints

- Go to a farm where you can "pick your own." Bring home the pickings and cook them. Pumpkins are especially good for this: you can roast the seeds, make pumpkin bread or pie from the pulp, and use the shell as a Halloween jack-o-lantern.
- Read *Daisy's Garden* by Mordecai Gerstein and Susan Yard Harris (Hyperion, 1995).

17 Garbage Analysis

Helps develop: understanding of research methods, ability to make generalizations from details, sorting and categorizing skills

Through archaeology we learn about ancient peoples—and about ourselves.

You'll Need newspaper; rubber or surgical gloves; the contents of a household garbage can

Before You Begin Ask your child to help you empty the garbage.

What to Do

1 Spread a layer or two of newspaper on the floor or in the yard. Use this as a surface for laying out the garbage and sorting it. Put gloves on yourself and your child.

2 Invite your child to remove something from the garbage and talk about why it's there. "I wonder why we aren't keeping this."

3 As you and your child remove more objects, encourage him to sort them into piles. "Is that like anything else we've found? What's alike about them?" Let your child create his own categories and name them, for example, food scraps, paper, packaging, junk mail, and so forth.

4 Once all the garbage is sorted, encourage your child to make statements about what the garbage shows. "Hmm. What do we throw out most in this family? Why is there so much paper in this garbage can?" And so on.

Follow-up Activities

• Talk about what makes garbage garbage. Why don't people want things? Is garbage bad? Is wearing gloves really necessary? Why or why not?

- Explore other garbage cans in different rooms in your house. Compare and contrast, and wonder together about the differences and similarities.

- Assess your system of garbage disposal. Talk about where your garbage will wind up. Determine, with your child, whether your household can create less garbage. Work together with your child to find solutions to the too-much-garbage problem: create a compost heap, create a scrap paper box from used paper and junk mail, and so on.

What's Happening	*It's sometimes the things we don't think about that reveal the most about us. A family that throws out a lot of paper might do a lot of writing. A family who throws out a lot of tissues might have colds or allergies. By studying garbage, you can tell a lot about people. You can also make generalizations about the community or society in which the people live. If there's a lot of packaging material in your garbage can, you can wonder with your child why people work so hard to create materials that just get thrown away—and why customers buy them. If there are a lot of food scraps or vegetable scrapings, you can wonder if there's a more efficient way to use them.*

Moving Ahead Find out where your garbage goes. How is each individual piece handled? How much does your garbage weigh? How much does it cost you to dispose of it? See Activity 15: Behind the Scenes for suggestions of ways to find out more about the process of garbage disposal.

Helpful Hint Visit a museum and look at some of the relics of other cultures. Find out with your child where and how these relics were found. What do these objects tell about the people who used them? Help your child understand that to learn about people, archaeologists consider both the things people valued—their treasures, carefully kept and protected—and the things that people threw out.

18 Helter Shelter

Helps develop: understanding that shelter is a basic human (and animal) need, building and planning skills

Everybody needs to be warm and dry.

You'll Need   various materials for creating a shelter (branches, boughs, lengths of fabric or blankets, etc.); chairs, blankets, pillows, etc.

Before You Begin   Talk with your child about different homes—those of other people, and those that animals make.

What to Do

1   Invite your child to imagine that the two of you are in the middle of the wilderness. What would you need to survive?

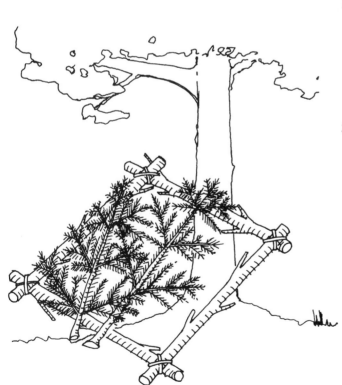

2   Talk about the needs your child suggests. Why is each one important? Could you truly not survive without each? Talk about shelter as a place to keep warm and dry. Say, "I wonder how we could make a shelter with what's around here."

3   Follow your child's lead in planning a shelter, gathering materials, and building and furnishing a structure. Encourage her to try her ideas and to think of new solutions to problems if one idea doesn't work out. Talk about each aspect of the building—basic structure, windows, doors, floor, furnishings— and how it contributes to the shelter.

Follow-up Activities	• Share a meal or spend a night in your shelter.
	• Talk about how your shelter would have to change if someone were really going to live there and how it would have to change with the seasons.

What's Happening	It's important for children to understand that all people need shelter. It's one of the essential needs that people share. Through imagining what it would be like to exist without her familiar house or apartment, your child gains insight into what shelter really is and why it's necessary.

Moving Ahead	Take a look at all the different kinds of people (and animal) shelters that exist in the world. Children are fascinated by different kinds of housing, including tents, igloos, huts, and other shelters that humans around the world have devised over the centuries. As your child learns about other cultures and times, encourage her to find out about housing.
Helpful Hint	Read *A House Is a House for Me* by Mary Ann Hoberman (Viking, 1978).

19 How to Cut a Sandwich

How to Cut
a Sandwich

Helps develop: *flexibility in thinking, problem-solving skills, cooperation, respect for others*

There's more than one way to skin a cat.

You'll Need sandwich of any kind; cutting board; table knife and fork; bread knife, *or* cookie cutters

Before You Begin Invite your child to help you make sandwiches and other simple meals.

What to Do

1 Make a sandwich and leave it whole on the cutting board. Say to your child, "I wonder what I can do to make this sandwich easier for you to eat. It's too big to put in your mouth all at once."

2 With your child, develop a list of possible ways to make the sandwich smaller, such as cutting it with a table knife and fork, cutting it in half or diagonally with a bread knife, or using cookie cutters to make bite-size pieces.

3 Invite your child to choose one idea for today. Let him help you cut the sandwich that way.

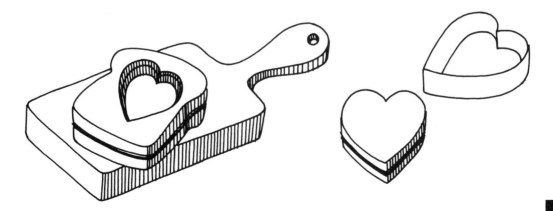

Follow-up Activity   Over the next few days, try new sandwich-cutting techniques. Evaluate them all with your child. Which does he like best? Why? Once you've chosen the way you and your child like best, encourage him to have an accepting attitude toward other ways and to try them from time to time just for fun.

What's Happening   A child who goes to school or visits a friend's house often encounters new ways of doing things. Some children come home and say, "They didn't do it right." Through this activity, and variations that allow your child to see that there are many possible solutions to one basic problem, you can help your child respect and accept new ways as different, not wrong.

Moving Ahead   Follow this procedure with all sorts of household problems, big and small: how to lay out a garden, how to fit dishes into a cupboard, how to "do" hair, and so on.

Helpful Hint   Take a walk or drive home a new way. How many ways can you and your child find to get from your house to a friend's? To the brook? To the subway?

20 Coded Communication

You know what I mean?

You'll Need   paper, pencils, and crayons (optional); sticks or rocks (optional); library resources

Before You Begin   Encourage your child to see different forms of communication, for example, that a red light means stop.

What to Do

1 Ask your child to think of ways to communicate without speaking or writing or signing. Discuss ideas she comes up with.

2 Talk to your child about codes: a code is a system of symbols or actions that stand for words and phrases. Describe Morse code—long and short sounds that stand for letters. If you can, demonstrate the Morse code for SOS by rapping on a table: • • • — — — • • • (three short, three long, and three short raps).

3 Invite your child to think up a code with you. Some suggestions:

- Devise a variation on Morse code that you make by knocking. One knock means hello, and so on.

- Use colors to show moods. You might ask your child, "How are you?" and she might answer with a color that you've both decided stands for a feeling.

- If your child writes, have her think of symbols that stand for words (as in a rebus) or letters.

- Play hide-and-seek with code. Use sticks or rocks to point the way to a hiding place, or assign places to different numbers of rocks; for example, two rocks means the back porch.

4 Use your code with your child. Make changes as needed.

Follow-up Activity   Use library resources to find examples of code systems to share with your child: semaphore; nautical flags, in which different colors and patterns stand for letters; backward alphabet code (A stands for Z, B stands for Y, etc.). Talk about why people need to use codes.

What's Happening   Through this activity, you and your child get closer to the purpose of communication between people: to give directions, to express views, to negotiate, and to share. By making up your own code together, you help your child to grasp the concept of what a symbolic language is and how people put it together.

Moving Ahead   Introduce your child to the idea of jargon: words or sets of words that are used by people in specific fields to talk about things within that field. Often, people outside the field are confused by jargon and can't understand what they're hearing. There are words, for example, for every part of a car, for the way children relate to each other in school, for weather, and so on. Let your child see you wonder about the meanings of jargon words and model for her how to ask questions and use sources to find out what these words mean.

Helpful Hint   Read *Communication* by Aliki (Greenwillow, 1993).

PART TWO

We're in This Together

How many hats do you wear? How many people are you? One person (and I am such a person) can be a grandma, mother, teacher, shopper, writer, TV watcher, golfer, and so on. Children have their own different roles: son or daughter, playmate, friend, cousin, and so forth. In this section—the social studies section—children explore the needs and deeds of people in their society, through finding out how people talk about themselves and through sharing stories. Empathy, citizenship, cooperation, and collaboration begin at home, through these activities that encourage making connections with others. Here, too, are ideas for helping your child move out into the community, neighborhood, classroom, and nation, with a personal understanding of his own abilities and responsibilities.

21 The Different Journal

Journal

Helps develop: *concepts of comparison and contrast, empathy, self-expression*

If Alice had kept a journal during her trip through Wonderland, things might still have been "curiouser and curiouser," but they might have been easier to cope with.

You'll Need   pencil or pen; notebook; a string; photographs and postcards (optional)

Before You Begin   Use this activity when you're planning a stay at a relative's or friend's house, or anyplace that is new or strange to your child.

What to Do   **1** As you talk to your child about the place you'll be visiting together, mention that he'll be seeing some new and different things. Talk about what some of these might be. Included in this discussion might be some of the special "rules" about being at Aunt Esther's house, at the beach, in a big city, and so on.

2 Suggest that your child keep track of differences—including words, attitudes, sights, and so on—between your destination and home. Tie a pencil or pen to a notebook with string, then give him the notebook. Encourage your child to draw or write down things that are different.

3 As you travel, talk with your child about the differences between home and where you are. Encourage your child to express his feelings about the differences.

Follow-up Activities
- Back home again, invite your child to share his journal with friends.
- Help your child add souvenir photographs and postcards to the journal.

What's Happening *It might seem as though keeping a journal of differences might put the focus of your trip on making comparisons. The fact is, your child is going to notice differences anyway, and will be affected by them—especially differences in people's behavior and attitudes. This journal gives your child a forum to identify those differences, write about them, and discuss them with you. As you talk together, you can get into the whys behind the differences. Your attitude toward this process will help determine whether your child grows up saying "Vive la différence!" or "Eew. Weird!"*

Moving Ahead You can encourage your child to keep a journal of differences in any situation—school, joint custody, day care, a new baby.

Helpful Hint Before you travel, do Activity 8: Eat Your Way through Cultures. Then, when you travel, hunt down new and different ways to eat. Encourage your child to try new things and to write about them in his journal.

22 Being a Thing

Helps develop: cooperation skills, feeling for drama and dance, understanding of form and function

"I'm a little teapot, short and stout."

You'll Need you and your child; costumes and props(optional); other children or adults

Before You Begin Encourage your child to playact, pretending to be someone— or something—else.

What to Do

1 Invite your child to "be" something with you: a car with a driver, a teapot and a teacup, a toaster and toast, or a machine that has integrated parts, such as a mixer, a dump truck, a lamp.

2 Ask your child what part of the thing she'd like to be. The bulb in the lamp? The beaters of the mixer? How will she play this part? What will she have to do?

3 What does your child want you to be? Ask if she has any suggestions as to how you should play your part.

4 Work together to act out your parts and be the thing. Then consult with one another about ways to improve or refine your performance.

5 Be the thing together for an audience.

Follow-up Activity Invite other people to get involved. Encourage your child to make this a spontaneous activity and let other people jump in. "I'll be the bowl!" "You be the spatula and take the batter out of the bowl!" "We need someone to be the cook and turn the mixer on."

Moving Ahead   Charades is a great game for getting children not only to put themselves in the place of others and to communicate clearly, but also to interpret the actions and ideas of others. First, play in only one category, such as storybook characters, and limit the interpretation to figuring out characters by movement, words, or attitudes. Eventually move up to the more adult version of the game, in which titles, syllables, and rhymes are used as well as actions and gestures.

Helpful Hint   David Macaulay's book *The Way Things Work* (Houghton Mifflin, 1988) and the accompanying CD-ROM kit can give you the information you need to help your child understand the workings of machinery.

23 The Way I Heard It...

Helps develop: *understanding of oral history, respect for individuality, flexibility in thinking*

So, Cinderella's fairy godmother found three white rats—or were they mice?—in the garden and turned them into footmen—or were they horses?— with a swoosh of her magic wand . . . .

You'll Need tape recorder with microphone; other children or adults; film version of at least one well-known fairy tale or folktale (optional)

Before You Begin Be sure your child is familiar with well-known fairy tales or folktales.

What to Do

1 Wonder with your child where stories come from. Talk about the now-famous people who went around writing down stories that folks were telling at the time when printed books became popular, such as Joseph Jacobs in England and the Brothers Grimm in Germany. Help your child to see that many favorite stories were passed down by word of mouth.

2 Say, "I wonder if the stories are still changing." Your child may already have some ideas about this, if he has read, for example, Trina Schart Hyman's version of *Snow White* and seen the Disney movie.

3 Invite your child to tell the story in his own words, using the tape recorder.

4 Next suggest that your child invite other people to tell the story in their own words into the tape recorder. Storytellers should be encouraged to use drama and detail in their tellings.

5 Play the tape. What was similar about each telling? What was different?

Follow-up Activities
- Ask other people to add to the tape.
- Do the same activity with another well-known story.
- Look at book and film versions of the story to extend the comparison.

What's Happening

Not only is your child getting an idea of where stories (and books and movies) come from, he's forming concepts about how people take in information and then communicate it. He may notice that individuals reveal their values, backgrounds, experiences, dramatic talents, and sense of humor in their stories.

Moving Ahead   Talk about the times and places in which stories were passed along solely through storytellers. What were those times like? What did people wear? Where did they live?

Helpful Hint   Here are several versions of just one folktale:
- *Snow White and the Seven Dwarfs* by Jacob Grimm and Wilhelm K. Grimm, translated by Randall Jarrell (Farrar, Straus & Giroux, 1972)
- *Snow White* by Jacob Grimm and Wilhelm K. Grimm, translated by Paul Heins (Little, Brown, 1979)
- *Walt Disney's Snow White and the Seven Dwarfs* adapted by Denise Lewis Patrick (Western, 1992)

24 Host and Guest

*The best manners are those that
make other people comfortable.*

You'll Need you and your child

Before You Begin Talk with your child about your house "rules" and how they might be different from another family's house rules.

What to Do

1 Ask your child to talk about what happens when a friend comes to visit. Talk about some of the things two friends might do together. Ask your child to suggest uncomfortable situations that can arise when one person visits another.

2 Role-play one of the difficult situations your child suggests. Invite her to play the host or the guest; you play the other part.

3 Play the situation out several different ways. After the first time, go back and discuss what happened. What could one of you have said or done differently to make things better for both? Try playing the roles as if you were a shy guest, a selfish host, a grabby guest, a host whose pet scared the guest, and anything else you can think of.

Follow-up Activities

- Work with your child to come up with a list of rules of thumb to keep in mind when having a friend over or visiting a friend's house. "A good guest is . . ." and "A good host is . . ."

- Encourage your child to make up if-then statements to resolve sticky situations that might arise, for example, "If I don't want to share my teddy bear, then I'll put it away before my friend comes."

Moving Ahead   Try other getting-along activities such as Activity 27: Meet Me Halfway, Activity 30: Playing by Your Own Rules, and Activity 34: Shake Hands.

Helpful Hint   Conflicts often arise when people have different expectations. In my daughter's best friend's family, the birthday girl goes first in all the games and gets the first piece of cake. In my family, the birthday girl goes last (and can't win prizes) in games, and serves the cake, serving herself last. This was one of the earliest conflicts my daughter and her friend had to resolve. They did it by simply stating rules: "At your house . . ." or "When it's your birthday . . ." By watching and respecting each other's differences, each came to see the value of the other's way of doing things. You can help your child understand others' ways of doing things—and how play dates can play out in various situations—through these books:

- *Jamaica and Brianna* by Juanita Havill (Houghton Mifflin, 1993)

- *Best Friends for Frances* by Russell Hoban (HarperCollins, 1976)

- *Let's Be Enemies* by Janice May Udry (HarperCollins, 1961)

25 Smash Ball

Keep it up!

You'll Need 2 or more players; a bouncy playground ball or, for younger children, a balloon

Before You Begin Give your child plenty of opportunities to play with balls and balloons.

What to Do 1 Have the players stand together. One person holds the ball.

2 Everyone counts to three. On the count of three, the ball is tossed into the air.

3 Players take turns batting the ball into the air, keeping it from touching the ground. No player should hit the ball more than twice in a row.

4 The game ends when players get tired or the ball hits the ground.

Follow-up Activities
- Develop your own new and goofy ways to play Smash Ball—hit the ball with only your foot, or hit a balloon with only your head or bottom.
- Develop your team's own personal best. How many times can the team hit the ball and keep it in the air?

What's Happening *The team is working together to reach a common goal. Instead of competing against each other to see which player is best, each player plays his or her own best for the good of the team. The results don't really matter. A game like this keeps the focus on having fun, running around, and laughing and yelling, not on showing individual prowess.*

Moving Ahead   With any sport, especially ones in which your child may play competitively, take time to play noncompetitively, just for fun. For example, say you're playing baseball. Count no foul balls, and outlaw strikeouts. Change the rules, goof around, and let every child experience running bases, swinging the bat, and throwing the ball. A relaxed child will have a good time and may become stronger, more ready to excel when it's time once again to play competitively.

Helpful Hint   Competitive parents raise competitive children. What parents can do to help their children be happy whether or not they're competitive is to role-play situations that might arise on the playing field. Together, come up with maxims or rules of thumb for dealing with praise, put-downs, overcompetitiveness, victory, and defeat.

26 What Did Goldilocks Think of the Three Bears?

Helps develop: understanding of different points of view and how people form opinions and attitudes

I was tired and hungry, and they had warm beds and warm food.

You'll Need   storybook; paper and pencil (optional)

Before You Begin   Read to your child whenever possible. Read her favorite stories over and over.

What to Do

1 Pick a story that your child knows well. Talk with her about the feelings of the character from whose point of view the story is told. For example, say something like, "You know, I was thinking about Goldilocks and the Three Bears. Those Bears sure were mad at her . . . ."

2 Pretend to be a news reporter interviewing Goldilocks. Say, "I wonder whether Goldilocks [the other character] would tell this story." Suggest that your child pretend she's Goldilocks. Ask, "Can you tell us what happened to you today? How do you feel about the Bears whose house you visited?"

3 Talk about your child's character's view of the story and discuss how it's different from the way the story is usually told. How would Goldilocks feel about the story? How might the story have come to be told the way that it is?

Follow-up Activities
- Suggest that your child retell or rewrite the story from her character's point of view.
- Play this game with other stories your child has read with you.
- As you read new stories together, talk about the characters' points of view. Look at illustrations and talk about the expressions or attitudes of the characters shown.

What's Happening This activity makes it fun and interesting to look at life from a different standpoint—that of another person. Empathizing is a valuable experience, an important part of learning to cooperate with and appreciate other people. It's so easy to say that Goldilocks was bad, a spoiled brat who just took whatever she wanted. The story sounds completely different when told from the point of view of a hungry, cold, tired child. This activity also leads your child to a clearer understanding of character, an asset in her writing and dramatic development.

Moving Ahead If your child comes home from a play date, day care, or school with a tale about something another child did, first sympathize, then try gently to encourage your child to play out the roles of the children involved. Invite her to take on new roles and to empathize with each child in the situation.

Helpful Hint Help your child to create a play or puppet show of the story, telling it twice or more, once from each point of view.

27 Meet Me Halfway

27 Meet Me Halfway

Helps develop: *interpersonal skills, understanding of mediator's role, respect for another's point of view*

This classic method of mediation empowers your child to resolve emotional situations with other children. It can also be your key to keeping your head when those about you are losing theirs.

You'll Need 2 squabbling children

Before You Begin Encourage your child to put her feelings into words when she's upset.

What to Do

1 Enter the room. Listen to what the kids say about the disagreement. When you feel you have a rudimentary grasp of the problem that is causing the squabble, get the attention of the children involved.

2 Address the squabblers directly, one at a time. Tell each child what, in your view, his or her problem is. "Sam, it seems to me that you want all the crayons. You're mad because Lauren wants to draw too."

3 Make sure the first child agrees that you've clearly stated his or her problem before moving on to the other child. Ask the first child to add to your assessment of the situation if the child feels it is necessary.

4 Follow the same procedure for the second child.

5 Ask, "Can you see any way to negotiate this problem?" Explain what the word *negotiate* means (find a solution that will make both parties happy). Encourage them to think of a few solutions and to decide together which to follow. If they need help, offer a few suggestions: split the crayons, take turns using all the crayons, find something else to do together.

6 Do not impose a solution. Insist that the former squabblers choose their own solution and implement it together.

Follow-up Activities

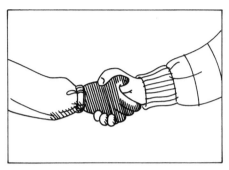

- Solve conflicts between you and your child in a similar manner, using them as opportunities to model problem solving for and with your child.

  - Use hypothetical situations or arguments you and your child overhear at the playground as material to discuss how problems might be mediated and solved.

  - Encourage your child to take on the mediator's role.

  - Once children understand the mediator's role, you can offer to help, ("Do you want a mediator?") and allow them to decide whether to accept your offer or to solve the conflict themselves.

What's Happening This mediation method won't stop squabbles from happening again, but it will help the children involved in squabbles to state their positions clearly, see how their needs and wants relate to others', and find not just one but several potential solutions to each problem. Mediation is an important part of life and will be a vital skill for the adults of the future.

Moving Ahead What happens when conflicts aren't resolved? Now that your child has experience and practice seeing two sides of a conflict and suggesting solutions, he can more readily understand larger, global issues in the same light. If you watch the news together and try to help your child interpret what he sees and hears, you can guide him to see the different sides of issues.

Helpful Hints
- In my dealings with children, I use "real" terms, such as *conflict, solution, negotiate, mediate.* Putting a name on an idea helps make it more solid for children and also gives them steps to pass through in the process of negotiating a conflict.

- Peer mediation, a trend in middle and high schools, clearly has its place in primary and preschool classes. While parents don't always feel free to become involved in classroom management, they can make suggestions to teachers or simply inform them that their children are accustomed to resolving problems through peer mediation.

28 Slap Hands

This activity—part of adult sensitivity training— lets children feel one another's energy as they get out their own feelings. No one gets hurt. It's the Golden Rule ("Do unto others . . .") in physical terms.

Helps develop: understanding of relationship between emotions and physical actions, problem-solving skills, interpersonal skills

You'll Need 2 angry children; pillows *or* paper and pencils (optional)

Before You Begin Use situations in books, television shows, and real life as spring-boards to a discussion of anger and ways people handle it.

What to Do
1 When children become angry with one another, ask them, "Do you two want to play Slap Hands?"

2 Lay the ground rules: Participants can slap palms of hands only—no fists, and no pulling away. The most important rule is: "You can hit my hands as hard as you want, but I can hit your hands just as hard in return."

3 Demonstrate by doing Slap Hands with someone else. Both children will see the importance of slapping only as hard as they're comfortable being slapped back.

4 Have the children agree that they must determine together when to stop, and that the rules must be followed to the letter.

5 Let the younger or smaller child go first. The older child holds out the palms of his or her hands (in either high-five or low-five position), and the younger child lets fly.

6 The older child then slaps the younger child's hands, no harder than the younger child slapped him or her. This goes on until both players agree to stop.

Follow-up Activities
• Encourage the children to talk about how this game makes them feel and whether it helps them assuage their anger.

- When children get into an argument or just get angry, encourage them to hit pillows, draw their feelings on paper, or run off their negative energy on a playground or in the backyard.

What's Happening   *S*mall children with big feelings need to find ways to let off steam without harming those around them. Slap Hands serves this purpose, with a major difference: it allows two children who are angry, bored, or annoyed with one another *to get out their frustration* together. *The palms of both parties sting equally.*

Moving Ahead   You can help children develop consideration for one another by suggesting that they wash each other's faces or brush each other's hair, and take turns being leader and helper with chores. (But not while they're still angry!)

Helpful Hint   Encourage children to find fair solutions to other problems, such as these:

- Who gets the big piece? When there's something to be shared between two children, have one do the cutting and the other do the distributing. Watch how fairly things get split!
- A child who doesn't want to share something gets permission to draw that line, as long as he or she offers to share something else instead.

29 Big Bad Wolf in the A & P

What would happen if . . . ?

You'll Need   at least one storybook version of *The Three Little Pigs* or *Little Red Riding Hood*

Before You Begin   Read at least one version of *The Three Little Pigs* or *Little Red Riding Hood* with your child.

What to Do   **1** Say to your child, "Let's think about what would happen if the Big Bad Wolf went to our grocery store."

2 Together, make up a story about the chaos that might result; for example, the Wolf might try to eat all the ice cream, chase all the children, blow displays down, leave without paying, and so on.

3 Laugh it up; make it vivid and silly. Ask, "And then what would he say?" Encourage your child to imagine how the Wolf would look and sound, and how people would respond to him.

Follow-up Activity Talk about what Little Red Riding Hood or the Three Little Pigs should do the next time they meet the Wolf.

What's Happening *By putting a familiar character into a new situation, you help your child to understand personality and motivation. Children who practice understanding someone's feelings or perspective can interpret others' actions as well. This ability will add to your child's sense of other cultures, and will serve him well in the classroom community.*

Moving Ahead For some, the next logical step would be to teach "stranger danger" to your child. I disagree with the premise behind such lessons—that bad things happen only through strangers. Rather, I advise you to use this activity as a lead-in to role-playing about dealing with someone who acts like the Big Bad Wolf or who in any way oversteps the bounds of appropriate social behavior. Give your child practice on an everyday basis in resolving conflicts, speaking for himself, solving problems, being treated respectfully by adults, and saying no to adults.

Helpful Hints Here are a few Big Bad Wolf books:

- *The True Story of the Three Little Pigs* by Jon Scieszka (Viking, 1989)
- *Three Little Pigs* by David McPhail (Scholastic, 1995)
- *Little Red Riding Hood* by Jacob Grimm and Wilhelm K. Grimm, illustrated by Trina Schart Hyman (Holiday, 1983)
- *Little Red Riding Hood* by William Wegman (Hyperion, 1993)

30 Playing by Your Own Rules

Helps develop: *ability to plan a process, concept of fairness, flexibility*

Play your own way.

You'll Need board game of any kind

Before You Begin Play age-appropriate board games with your child.

What to Do

1 Ask your child, "So, what rules do we want to play by?"

2 Your child may recite the official rules to you. Ask, "Is that okay with you?" If the answer is yes—and the rules are clear to both of you—then go ahead and play. If your child answers no, ask, "What bothers you about this game? How could we change it to make it more fun?"

3 Take your child's suggestions. Try playing the game her way. Talk about how the game feels when played under these new rules. What else could be changed? Which way is more fun?

4 Continue playing the game, altering rules and procedures as you go. One way to consider changing the game is to change the objective. Some possibilities include

- helping each other win together, instead of competing;
- playing a game like Chutes and Ladders or Candy Land in such a way that you can't ever get sent back; or
- limiting the number of rounds or setting a time period to protect your (or your child's) sanity.

Follow-up Activity

- Name your game's new rules. In the future, when you play that game, agree on the kind of rules you'll play by.

People sometimes get locked into rigid procedures when it comes to games (not to mention sports). Through this activity, you can remind your child that the point of playing games is to enjoy yourself, and that if you're not enjoying yourself, you can change the game to suit you. Mention the fact that people made up this store-bought board game in the first place; they were doing what pleased them. Even though they may have tried the game out on real, live kids, there may still be room for improvement.

The ability to think flexibly is key to problem solving. Often the best solution to a dilemma is to throw out the customary procedure, open wide the doors to fresh air, and think of a completely new approach. Through activities like this, your child is prepared to do just that.

Moving Ahead What does your child like best about this game? Could you create your own game that uses the best aspects of several games together? Encourage your child to create a game board, pieces, and procedures for an original new game.

Helpful Hint Go right ahead and try those heavily advertised board games your child sees on television—in moderation. Play it their (the manufacturer's) way if you want, then revise the game to suit your child's own way of playing. Use these kinds of games, too, as an opportunity to discuss truth in advertising and to assess aspects of a toy that are hyped—and how.

31 Anybody Can Do Anything

Would you want to be depicted that way?

You'll Need radio or television programs, books, magazines, or other sources of pictures and stories that show, in various lights, people of both sexes and of a variety of races and cultures, as well as people with disabilities; library resources

Before You Begin Try to expose your child to other cultures as often as possible.

What to Do

1 When you hear someone (or a group of people) knocked or stereotyped because of race, religion, nationality, profession, or sex, see it as an opportunity to debunk stereotypes. You might hear a radio ad in which a spokesman for a Mexican restaurant speaks with an accent and demeanor that could only have been inspired by Speedy Gonzales. Or you might see portrayals of a woman being helpless with tools or a man who can't do the simplest tasks in the kitchen.

2 Ask your child, "Why is that man talking like that?" or "Why can't these people do these things?" With your child, describe the accent, the vocabulary, the statements being made, or the assumptions about gender roles.

3 Talk about the group that's being stereotyped. For Mexicans, for example, wonder together what it's like in Mexico, how people really behave there, and share information about it with your child. Say, "If you were Mexican,

how would you feel if you heard this commercial?" Guide your child to see that Mexicans don't talk like this; help him to see that exaggeration of a characteristic such as accent is insulting.

Follow-up Activities

- With your child, check out advertisements for their portrayals of groups of people.

- Watch television. Be alert to stereotypical characterizations in stories and on TV. Ask, "Do you think all —— people act like that?"

- Continually point out and ask your child to evaluate images. Encourage him to analyze the motives of the people who create these images.

- Go to the library with your child. Look for books about the people in question. Find books that show girls using carpentry tools, Native Americans without feathers and teepees, children in wheelchairs living active, involved, independent lives. Talk about the images you find in the books, including those that are stereotypical. Ask, "Would you want to be depicted this way? Why do you think the person who made this book showed people this way?"

What's Happening

This activity helps your child to think for himself and to evaluate portrayals of people rather than accept them as reality. Making your child aware of stereotypes is key to making him open and curious about every individual and every individual situation.

A friend's six-year-old daughter received a birthday present that really turned her mother's stomach: a game that involved gathering jewelry. The winner gained a crown and became a princess, while black jewelry was conferred on losers, who remained commoners. The game was chock-full of stereotypes, from the blonde little girls on the box lid to the black-is-bad ring inside. Still, the game was an eye-opener. Children of color, boys included, were equally enthusiastic about winning jewels. What made the difference was how they played the game: questioning the assumptions of its creators as they went along while at the same time accepting all participants as potential winners.

Moving Ahead   Continue to share your thoughts about stereotypes with your child, moving away from his immediate concerns and circle of friends to address images of people with whom your child has not had much contact. Encourage him to see people as individuals through activities such as Activity 2: Wrappers! and Activity 8: Eat Your Way through Cultures.

Helpful Hint   Try these stereotype-busting books:
- *Black Is Brown Is Tan* by Arnold Adoff (HarperCollins, 1992)
- *Amazing Grace* by Mary Hoffman (Dial, 1991)
- *Stay Away from Simon!* by Carol Carrick (Clarion, 1985)

32 The Democratic Process

Helps develop: understanding of voting process and what it shows about a group, math and graphing skills

I will never forget the day in 1969 when we took a vote during a car trip in New York State. The issue? Whether to take a side trip to a big rock-music concert just south of Albany. The outcome? The kids voted themselves out of Woodstock.

You'll Need several paper cups or other similar-size containers; marking pen; pencils; index cards; paper

Before You Begin Talk with your child about opinions, encouraging her to form her own and express them.

What to Do

1 Pick an issue, any issue, such as what to have for dinner. Say, "I wonder how this group stands on the subject of dinner."

2 Accept nominations from the floor. "Do I have any nominations for what to have for dinner tonight?"

3 Label each cup with one nomination. (In this case, you may want to include only choices that you have on hand.)

4 Have each person write his or her name on an index card.

5 Let each person vote by placing his or her index card in the appropriate cup.

6 When everyone has voted, tally the votes by lining up the index cards beside each cup. Which has the most?

Follow-up Activities Try these other ways of taking a vote:

- Voters use a ballot that lists all nominations. Ballots are tallied.
- Voters raise their hands for the nomination they want.
- Voters say aye for the nomination they want.
- This method is more complicated, but it's practical and fun. Say you've just started vacation and everybody wants to do something different. Make enough cards for each nomination so that each person has a complete set. Take a vote each day by asking voters to hold up the card for the activity they want the group to do. Have everyone hand in their cards for the winning nomination. Eventually, each person's nomination will win.

What's Happening Your child is getting a firsthand, hands-on, meaningful experience with the idea that each person gets one vote and that each person's vote carries equal weight. For this reason, don't have your family vote in situations that are best decided diplomatically rather than democratically. (My children still insist I should have been despotic about going to Woodstock.) As much as possible, involve your child in family decisions. She'll gain confidence, respect for the opinions of others, and an understanding of the democratic process.

Moving Ahead Encourage your child to poll the people around her to learn their opinions and preferences on key matters. Show her different methods of graphing results: bar graphs, pie charts, and so forth. For ideas, try another book in this series, *Ready, Set, Count* (Wiley, 1995).

Helpful Hint Talk to your child about votes that you participate in or that are covered by news and other media.

33 The Bead Game

Helps develop: flexibility in thinking about customs and values

A version of this game is played in Literacy Volunteers of America workshops for teachers of English as a second language.

You'll Need a string of beads

Before You Begin Read, watch television, and make observations about other people with an attitude that *different* is wonderful, not weird.

What to Do **1** Ask your child what beads are good for. "How do you feel about beads? What can you do with them?"

2 Now ask your child to imagine that he comes from a far-away place where beads are given as gifts to loved ones. Tell your child that you're going to imagine that you come from another place, where beads are used as money to buy things. Think of names for your faraway places.

3 Walk up to your child with the beads in your hand. Point to something near the child or something he's wearing, say, his baseball cap. Give the beads to your child.

4 Remind your child to behave as someone from his faraway place would behave if given beads. (He might be flattered. He might hug you. He might thank you and walk away.)

5 Respond in character to your child's action. Remember, you want to buy something with those beads. (If he walks away, you might show anger.)

6 Stop and talk about what's going on. Each of you should explain your actions and come up with ways that you could resolve the misunderstanding.

Follow-up Activities • Talk about what happens when people have misunderstandings. What causes them? Is anyone really wrong? What can be done to avoid misunderstandings and to make peace if they occur?

- Consider what other meanings might people give to beads (decoration, game pieces, trail markers, etc.).

What's Happening

In this activity, you take an everyday object and give it new meaning that depends strictly on the imaginary culture you create. The door is open to new thoughts about customs and the way in which they develop. Don't stop with the beads. Go on to Moving Ahead for ideas of ways to extend this lesson to interpret customs from your own culture.

Moving Ahead

Here are some customs to discuss and consider with your child:

- In some countries, women must keep their heads and faces covered at all times. In other places, women must walk behind men.
- When Cherokee people make a decision, they choose what's best for most people. European Americans tend to think the needs of individuals are most important.
- In England, everyone bows or curtsies to the queen. Some American visitors refuse to bow or curtsy.

Helpful Hint

Try these books that get at the root of customs:

- *The Village of Round and Square Houses* by Ann Grifalconi (Little, Brown, 1986)
- *Dance at Grandpa's* by Laura Ingalls Wilder (HarperCollins, 1994)

34 Shake Hands

A handshake is worth a thousand words.

You'll Need you and your child; other people with whom to shake hands

Before You Begin Introduce your child to people, and other people to her.

What to Do

1 Give your child a demonstration of how to greet someone with a handshake. Do this by having your child play the part of the president, the head of the school, or someone else who may seem intimidating. Shake hands, look your child in the eyes, and say, "Hi, Mr. President."

2 Now ask your child to "play" herself, and you be someone else. (Let your child say who.) Encourage her to shake your hand firmly, look at you, and say, "Hello, ———."

3 Pretend to be someone who wants a big hug and kiss from your child. Point out that you (as this person) have just jumped out of a swimming pool and are dripping wet. Come toward your child as if to hug her. Suggest that your child avoid getting "wet" by sticking out her hand to shake.

Follow-up Activity Encourage your child to shake hands with people she meets at school, visitors who come to your home, and people in other places. Practice until shaking hands becomes second nature to your child.

A handshake is a great little item for your child to have in her repertoire of social skills. Adults find it adorable; what's more, it forces most adults to respect your child and see her as an individual. That dripping-wet, affectionate adult coming toward your child for a hug is obviously a metaphor for anybody your child doesn't want to—and shouldn't have to—hug or kiss. Note that at first when your child shakes hands she won't necessarily speak or even look at the other person. These can be actions to work up to.

Moving Ahead

Talk with your child about the social aspects of shaking hands. Here are a few that might come up in your conversation:

- In the old days, women didn't shake hands. They might have offered a hand for a kiss, however. Later in history, women still offered their hands for a handshake in the same position as the one for a kiss—supposedly to show that they were fragile and shouldn't be squeezed too hard.

- Some men (and women) think it's important to squeeze someone's hand really hard.

- Most people feel that you can tell a lot about a person from his or her handshake.

- Some people have developed their own special hand-shakes to mark them as members of a group. Some shake by linking pinkies or grabbing each other's thumbs. Boy Scouts shake by extending two fingers instead of the whole hand. Girl Scouts shake with their left hands while raising their right in the Girl Scout sig-nal (three fingers raised). What special handshake can you and your child devise?

Helpful Hint

When you're with your child in a location where many people are meeting each other (a train station, waiting room, or school open house, for example), watch together the way people greet each other. How many different ways can you spot?

35 Getting Active

*Volunteer. Write a letter. Paint a poster.
Speak up. Vote. Get involved!*

You'll Need materials determined by the situation

Before You Begin Talk with your child about something that's going on in your community.

What to Do

1 When you and your child see something in your community that makes you angry or sad, and that you feel should be changed, ask your child, "What do you think we could do about this?"

2 Consider your child's suggestions and suggest a few ideas of your own. Say you see a sidewalk that seems dangerously dark at night, rude graffiti, or a broken swing. You might consider writing a letter, making a phone call, contacting a local newspaper, painting over the graffiti, fixing the swing, and so on.

3 Decide on a plan. Put your plan into action. Involve your child as much as possible.

4 Wait for a response to your plan. Talk about your feelings about the response you get (including your feelings if you get no response).

Follow-up Activity Make activism a part of your everyday life with your child. Let him see you voting and participating at an adult level with activities associated with issues you feel strongly about, and continue to encourage him to do the same until he's old enough to write his own letters and make his own phone calls.

What's Happening   Through this activity you can help your child develop his notion of fairness to include issues that affect his life as a member of the community. When you do this on the neighborhood level, you help him develop strategies that he can then take into school and the larger community. While every action you take may not receive the response you and your child desire, your child will get important encouragement from you *that his thoughts and words are important, and he will feel empowered to speak up for himself and others in future situations.*

Moving Ahead   Find experiences for your child that allow him to see other people—kids and adults—standing up for what they believe in. These might include people in local parades, protesters, people on strike, door-to-door evangelists, and so on. Your attitude of respect and consideration for all people—and your courteous dissent toward those with whom you disagree—will teach your child a great deal.

Helpful Hint   Help your child to see the person behind bumper stickers, T-shirts, posters, billboards, and other printed expressions of opinion. Read the opinions with your child, talk about what they mean, and help your child consider them carefully.

PART THREE

A Whole World Out There

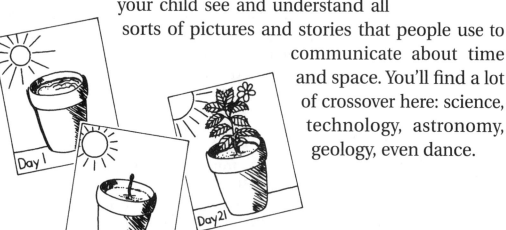

Some scientists and historians—and poets represent the relation of a person's life to the universe by saying that a person is but a grain of sand on the shores of time. That's one story, one explanation, one picture of the world.

These activities focus on helping your child see and understand all sorts of pictures and stories that people use to communicate about time and space. You'll find a lot of crossover here: science, technology, astronomy, geology, even dance.

36 Continent Book

elps develop: understanding of maps, relationship between natural world and a flat-map representation of the same

Where do you live?

You'll Need scissors; map *or* copy of map *or* jigsaw puzzle of the seven continents; tracing paper (optional); pencils; construction paper, fine sandpaper, fabric, or other sturdy material; paste; stapler; geography book

Before You Begin Dovetail this activity with others from Part One that involve learning about other cultures.

What to Do 1 Create a pattern of each continent for your child, in one of the following ways:

- Cut out the continents of a map.
  - Make a copy of a map and cut out the continents.
  - Trace around the continent pieces of a jigsaw puzzle and cut out the tracings.

2 Invite your child to trace each continent twice on a piece of construction paper, fine sandpaper, fabric, or other sturdy material.

3 Have your child paste one piece from each pair on a sheet of construction paper.

4 Staple the construction paper sheets together to make a book.

5 Encourage your child to match by shape the loose continent pieces to the pasted ones in her book.

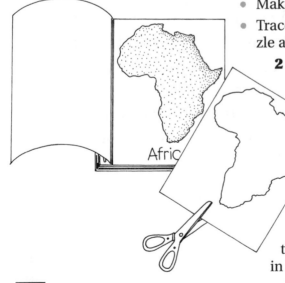

Follow-up Activities

- Help your child write the name of each continent on the appropriate page. Then have her match the continents by name.
- Using a geography book as a guide, begin to talk about the countries, terrain, climate, languages, and so forth of each continent.
- Help your child to lay out the seven continents as they are on a map. Consider the relative area of the world that is covered by land and the area covered by ocean.

What's Happening

This activity gives your child experience with the shape and relative size of the continents. The world is too complex to be represented as tiny pieces that represent countries. Instead, keep it simple at first by working with only the seven continents. If you cut the continents out of your paper map, your child can fit them back in to see their relationship with each other and with the oceans. Through the book and pieces—and much discussion about the real places they represent—your child will come to a more sure understanding of the meaning of maps. But remember, a young child doesn't readily get the fact that the small continent piece really represents a huge area.

Moving Ahead

To help your child grasp the names of the continents and their location in the world, move on to Activity 37: Tourist Spin.

Helpful Hint

Wooden puzzles of the world are available from Small World Toys.

37 Tourist Spin

Helps develop:
understanding of distances, transportation, geography, and cultures

I'm taking a boat to Africa to see giraffes.

You'll Need marking pen; paper plate; scissors; paper; paper brad; continent patterns created in Activity 36: Continent Book; game tokens borrowed from a board game *or* buttons or coins; rubber stamps or stickers; index cards

Before You Begin Do Activity 36: Continent Book, or be sure your child knows the names of the continents pretty well.

What to Do **1** Make the game.
- Label a paper plate with the names of the continents (Africa, Antarctica, Asia, Australia, Europe, North America, South America).
- Cut out a paper arrow and attach it to the plate with a paper brad so that the brad goes through the center of the arrow and the center of the plate. This is the spinner.

2 Play the game.
- Each player starts by placing his or her game token on a different continent.
- The first player announces where he or she is ("I'm in Africa"), then spins the spinner. The player announces his or her destination as indicated by the spinner ("I'm going to Australia"), then moves to that continent.
- Each player takes a turn. The game is over when one player (or all) has visited all of the continents.

Follow-up Activities
- Use a different rubber stamp or sticker to indicate a player's arrival on each continent. Have each player carry a "passport"—an index card folded in half—that gets "stamped" as the game progresses. The game is over when one player (or all) gets stamps or stickers from every continent.
- Try the variations listed in Moving Ahead.

What's Happening

By playing this game, your child gets a grasp of where each continent is situated on the globe and how it stands in relation to the oceans and to the other continents. Through the variations in Moving Ahead, he can gather information about climate, terrain, animals, and people, and even apply that knowledge to issues of transportation.

Moving Ahead   Supply each player with pieces of information concerning each continent. Then ask what he or she plans to do or see there. For example:
- "I'm traveling to Antarctica on an icebreaker to see the penguins."
- "I'm driving to South America to see the rain forest."

Helpful Hint   *The Facts on File Children's Atlas* by David Wright and Jill Wright (Facts on File, 1993) is a good source of pictures and information.

38 Plant a Timeline

To see a world in a grain of sand
And a heaven in a wild flower,
Hold infinity in the palm of your hand
And eternity in an hour.

—William Blake, "Auguries of Innocence"

You'll Need pictures of your child as a baby; seeds; flowerpot; soil; watering can; paper and pencils; tape or thumbtacks

Before You Begin Show your child pictures of herself as a baby and talk about how much she's changed.

What to Do

1 With your child, plant seeds in a flowerpot filled with soil, then add water. Place in a sunny spot.

2 Invite your child to help you make pictures to track the plant's growth. On one sheet of paper, suggest that your child draw the plant as it looks now (that is, with no signs of life). Post the drawing near the plant. Ask your child if she'd like to draw the plant every couple of days to show how it grows and changes.

3 Over the next few days, watch the plant closely with your child. Encourage her to draw it again if she likes. Post the drawings in order beside the first one.

Follow-up Activity   After your child's plant sprouts and grows, encourage her to record the dates of its life cycle, including when it blooms, flowers, makes fruit, drops its leaves, and even when it dies.

What's Happening   Through this activity your child will come to understand the life cycle of a plant: its progress over time from sprout to seedling to a plant that blossoms and fruits. If you do this outdoors in summer and allow the plant to die with the change of seasons, your child will see a more realistic life cycle than she would with a flower kept as a houseplant. What's key is not so much the understanding of time in specific segments, but the fact that living things change and develop over a period of time—an important concept in both social studies and science.

Moving Ahead   Do this activity with a baby animal (or a baby human!) as the subject. Your child can make her own baby book from the progression of pictures, including dates and commentary about the baby's growth. See Activity 39: Timeline of a Life.

Helpful Hint   For more planting and observing activities, see another book in this series, *Ready, Set, Explore* (Wiley, 1996).

39 Timeline of a Life

Imagine that the lives of friends and strangers alike could pass before you like pictures laid out in sequence on a table. How moving the march of time across those faces would be! What stories the pictures would tell!

Helps develop: *understanding of the aging process, history hooks for contemporary times, empathy and respect for individual differences*

You'll Need 6 to 12 pictures of one person (an adult) at various ages, from babyhood through adulthood; information through oral stories or books and magazine articles about the person; blank photo album, pen, and labels (optional); paper and pencils

Before You Begin Pick a person, any person: someone you know personally (and whose pictures you have or can borrow) or not (whose pictures you can get pictures from magazines or in books).

What to Do

1 Lay out the pictures on a tabletop in any order. Invite your child to look at the pictures with you.

2 Ask your child to choose a picture that he wonders about. Wonder together what the person was like at that age, what he or she did, where the person lived, and so on.

3 Try to find answers together. If it's someone you know, call the person up or bring him or her over to tell you stories. If it's someone who's no longer alive, see if you can find answers from a friend or family member. If it's someone famous, check book and magazine sources for information about the person at that age.

4 Work together with your child to put the pictures in chronological order and to gather a series of stories about the person.

5 Encourage your child to tell you the history of the person's life through the series of pictures.

6 Talk about the spaces—and corresponding stories—that fall between the pictures. "Here she is when she's three, and then again when she's ten. I wonder what she looked like . . . what happened to her . . . what she did . . . how she felt . . . in between."

Follow-up Activities

- Create an album of the person's life, with captions. See Activity 3: Every Picture Tells a Story.

- If you can't make an album of the pictures, write a narrative together about the person. Your child can illustrate the narrative with drawings of his own.

- Invite your child to share what he's discovered with others, retelling the stories in his own words.

What's Happening

This activity is a way to get a handle on a person's life— somebody real (Chief Joseph) or somebody fantastic (Big Bird), somebody distant (Great-Grandma, who never knew your child but would have loved to) or somebody close (a family friend). Your child will grasp important concepts of time and growth. Even more important, he'll gain an understanding of the rich variety that is possible in people's lives and of the kinds of happenings that change them.

Moving Ahead

With your child, read stories about real people's lives. As you read, try to trace character traits and experiences that formed strong themes in people's lives—things like honesty and trust (George Washington), the peaceable fight for justice (Martin Luther King, Jr.), and the need to be the voice of the "little guy" (Eleanor Roosevelt).

Helpful Hint

Read:

- *This Quiet Lady* by Charlotte Zolotow (Greenwillow, 1992)
- *Grandfather's Journey* by Allen Say (Houghton Mifflin, 1993)

40 Timeline of a Trip

Helps develop: relationship between time and events, concept of moving through a process

First we packed our suitcases . . .

You'll Need string; pencil; small spiral-bound sketchbook *or* 3-ring binder with looseleaf paper; glue stick; scissors; handheld pencil sharpener; small manila envelope

Before You Begin With your child, plan a trip to the mall, a visit to a museum, or a vacation.

What to Do
1 Talk to your child about the trip you're going to take together. Tell her that you want to help her remember important things about the trip, and that a timeline book will help.

2 Help your child set up a timeline book. Use string to tie a pencil to the spiral binding of the sketchbook or to one of the binder's rings. Put a glue stick, scissors, and a pencil sharpener in a manila envelope for use as needed.

3 As you travel, encourage your child to make drawings or write ideas about things she does and sees. Gather mementos to glue in as you go along (maps, tickets, photographs, etc.).

4 As you travel, look through the timeline book often to see (in progression) where you've been. Together, anticipate where you're going tomorrow and the next day.

Follow-up Activities
• Back home, encourage your child to share her timeline book with other people and to tell the story of the trip in chronological order.

• Make little timeline books of day trips.

- Use the timeline book idea for errand runs. Ask your child to make a list of things the two of you need to do, and then check them off, recording details of each stop as you go (or after you come home).

<table>
<tr><td>What's Happening</td><td>A very young child understands the concept of now. As the child grows, he or she grasps today and eventually understands the concepts of yesterday and tomorrow. Through this activity, you help your child to see a longer progression of yesterdays, todays, and tomorrows in relation to the everyday events of her own life. She gets practice looking back, looking around, and looking forward.</td></tr>
</table>

Moving Ahead It's fun to work with your child to create a timeline book, and also fascinating to create one of your own. If you have more than one child, encourage everyone to keep his or her own timeline book. Your entire family will be interested to see what grips each person most about the places you visit and the sights you see—and looking back at each person's timeline will help everyone remember more.

Helpful Hint A beautiful story about a trip timeline is found in *My Family Vacation* by Dayal Kaur Khalsa (Crown, 1988). May and her brother, mother, and father all experience their trip to Florida in a different way. Nostalgic illustrations of bygone American highways may trigger your own memories to share with your child.

41 Circular Calendar

Helps develop:
understanding of how time is represented and communicated, understanding of the patterns and rhythm of the seasons

We say time is linear, but we use a circular clock to represent it. We say the seasons go around, but we use a linear calendar to show a year. Here's a way to help your child understand how time and the seasons are a great big wheel that rolls on and on and on . . .

You'll Need
scissors *or* handsaw; drawing compass; poster board *or* wood; measuring stick; marking pen; yellow and 4 other colors of paint; paintbrush; bulletin board *or* picture-hanging kit; push-pin or thumbtack *or* 12 round-headed clothespins or dowels; tape or paste *or* pushpins; memorabilia of special occasions

Before You Begin
Talk with your child about the continuous flow of seasons, exploring the food, weather conditions, activities, and holidays that come with each season.

What to Do
1 Cut a circle of poster board or wood about 3 feet (1 m) in diameter.

2 Draw a circle about 1 foot (⅓ m) in diameter in the center of the cutout. Have your child color or paint the inner circle yellow to represent the sun.

3 Divide the outer ring into four equal sections to represent each of the seasons. Working in a clockwise direction, label each season and paint each a different color.

4 Divide each season section into three equal parts to represent the 12 months. Label each month.

5 If you're working with poster board, attach the calendar to a bulletin board with a thumbtack or pushpin through the top of the current month. If you're working with wood, use a dowel or clothespin to make a peg in the section for each month. Use a picture-hanging kit to hang the calendar to a wall at your child's eye level by the current month's peg.

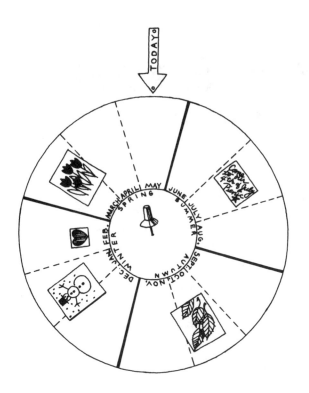

6 At the top of the bulletin board, pin an arrow labeled Today. Have your child turn the calendar counterclockwise to keep the current month and season at the top.

7 Talk with your child about the seasons and the months. Focus in on the time of year where you are now. Ask your child to create a drawing for the current month or season. Attach it to the appropriate place on the calendar.

8 Ask your child to recall a scene from last summer. Show him where that event would fall on the calendar. Then talk about something that might happen next summer. Demonstrate how the calendar will turn around to represent summer in the future.

Follow-up Activity   Continue to tape, paste, or tack drawings, holiday symbols, and announcements of special occasions on the calendar throughout the year and into the next.

What's Happening   For your child, the year starts now. With a circular calendar, that's always so. A circular calendar helps everyone—children included—to see the rhythm of the seasons and the way they flow from one to the next.

Moving Ahead   Have a "regular" calendar nearby for daily appointments. Help your child to see the relationship between the regular calendar and the circular one. How does each show his birthday? How does each show the months?

Helpful Hint   Sing Joni Mitchell's song "The Circle Game" with your child. Discuss the song's meaning. "The Circle Game" is from Mitchell's album *Ladies of the Canyon* (A&M) and also appears on the children's album *Hand in Hand: Songs of Parenthood* (Music for Little People).

42 Birthday Walk around the Sun

Helps develop: *understanding of time as related to earth's movement around sun, self-esteem, respect for others*

This is a fun and beautiful birthday-party activity for your child, whether with her family or a group of children. Let her take a walk for every year of her life.

You'll Need

sunrise and sunset to watch; birthday-party guests; a yellow ball or balloon; prepared speeches (stories) about each year of your child's life; photographs and drawings of each year of your child's life

Before You Begin

Watch the sunrise and sunset with your child. Talk with her about the sun's place in our lives.

What to Do

1 Have the guests sit in a circle. Ask one person to sit in the center, holding the yellow ball or balloon—the "sun."

2 Announce the birthday person. Have her stand in place for the first "speech," in which you give her name, her birth-date, and a little story about the day of her birth.

3 Say, "Then ——— began her walk around the sun." Have the birthday child walk around the outside of the circle and back to her place, while you give the second speech, telling about her first year of life. "She learned to roll over . . . to crawl . . . to say 'Dada.'" Show pictures of her first year.

4 Continue in this manner until your child has walked around the sun once for each year of her life. End with a wish for the coming year, and applause.

Follow-up Activities

• Talk about why you "walk around the sun" for every year of your life—to imitate the movement of the earth for every year.

• Talk about how time changes a child.

What's Happening   *This activity celebrates your child's life on earth by focusing on her relationship to the cosmos and on her special story—her life, her learning, her development and attributes. When you involve as many people as possible in recounting stories and giving speeches, sharing photographs and drawings, you make the experience truly a beautiful celebration for all.*

Moving Ahead   Help your child to understand the movement of the planets through space with Activity 43: The Dance of the Cosmos.

Helpful Hint   For a truly epic birthday celebration, involve your child in preparing a walk around the sun for a grandparent.

43 The Dance of the Cosmos

Helps develop: understanding of time's relation to the universe, understanding of relative position and movement of planets in solar system, sense of place in the universe

Turn a playground, some colored chalk, and a few rocks into a model of the universe for your five-to-seven-year-old.

You'll Need large concrete area that can be drawn on with chalk; several different colors of sidewalk chalk; 9 rocks, balls, or paper disks; other children

Before You Begin Look at the sun and moon. Talk about the earth as a giant ball moving through space.

What to Do

1 Invite your child to use one color of chalk to draw a big sun in the center of the concrete. Make it big! Make it bright! It has to shine all the way to the edges of the universe!

2 Tell your child the story of the sun: how it stays still in the center of the solar system while the planets move around it. Describe planets as great big rocks or balls of gas and rock that go around the sun.

3 Ask your child to use a different color of chalk to draw a path around the sun, moving carefully in a circle close to the sun. Talk about how it would feel to be so close to the sun (hot, dry). Give your child a rock, ball or paper disk to place on the path. Tell him the rock represents Mercury, the planet that follows this path.

4 Continue drawing paths and placing rocks for each of the other planets in the universe: Venus, Earth, Mars, Jupiter, Saturn, Neptune, Uranus, and Pluto. Talk about how close each planet is to the sun.

Follow-up Activity   If you have enough people on hand (this activity generally draws interested admirers), invite them to pick up a planet and trace its path around the sun by walking the chalked circle. "Look!" you can say to your child (and to everyone). "Look at all those planets dancing around the sun! You're one, and he's another!"

What's Happening   Of course, this activity is highly representational and doesn't come close to showing the relative sizes or distances of the planets and sun. But it gets across the point that there are planets circling around the sun, and that we're living on only one of them. As your child grows, he will hear the names of the planets often. Through this activity (and you should, of course, repeat it from time to time), he gains a frame of reference for understanding the solar system.

Moving Ahead   Use the star map in your newspaper to figure out what planets you can see in your night or early morning sky. Go out with your child to look. Wake him up early to see.

Helpful Hint   There are many wonderful materials and books about the planets and the sun on the market today. Here are just a few:

- solar system mobiles (various manufacturers)
- *The Magic School Bus Lost in the Solar System* by Joanna Cole (Scholastic, 1992)
- *The Sun's Family of Planets* by Allan Fowler (Children's Press, 1992)
- *The Earth and Sky* by Jean-Pierre Verdet (Scholastic, 1992)

44 Make Your Own Sundial

Helps develop:
understanding of
relationship of sun to
day and to passage of
time, math and
measurement skills

To make a sundial you can use a tree—or a pencil.

You'll Need
pencil, little statue, oblong stone that can stand on end, or similar object; sunny window *or* open outdoor area; paper and pencil (for indoor sundial) *or* rocks or sticks (for outdoor sundial); watch

Before You Begin
Talk about what life was like before electric light was invented. Discuss how people's reliance on sunlight shaped their days.

What to Do

1 Invite your child to explore with you how people kept time in the days before there were clocks. Begin the sundial by standing an object upright in a sunny place. This object is the gnomon, the part that casts a shadow. If you're inside by a sunny window, stand the gnomon in the middle of a sheet of paper. If you're outside, stand it in a bare spot where you can easily see the rock or sticks markers you'll put down.

2 Ask your child to notice where the sun is in the sky, and where the shadow from the object falls on the paper or ground. Inside, have her use a pencil to mark where the shadow falls on the paper. Outside, have her place a rock or stick on the place where the shadow falls.

3 Now check your watch. Inside, write the nearest hour on the paper. Outside, have your child mark it with an appropriate number of rocks or sticks (three for three o'clock).

4 Continue to check the shadows of your sundial at different hours and to add markings around it until you have a daylight clock around the gnomen. After this you and your child won't need to check your watch to see what time it is; you'll be able to check the sundial (on sunny days).

Follow-up Activities
- Use your sundial to plan activities with your child or to set time limits. "We'll go in when the sundial says four o'clock."
- Wonder with your child how people figured out the time from sundials before they had watches. Could timekeeping have been as precise then as it is now?

What's Happening   *You're helping your child to see the movement of the sun as a regular pattern. You're also showing your child how people use this movement to regulate their lives. Why do people need to know what time it is? Discussing this question with your child opens the door to an understanding of all sorts of human needs and experiences. Do animals need to tell time? How do they know when to go to sleep, to eat, to hunt? This question, too, will shed light on human behavior now and over the years.*

Moving Ahead   Check in a month or so to see whether your child's sundial still keeps time in the same way. How does it change with the seasons, and why?

Helpful Hint   Check garden supply stores and catalogs for sundials, which come in a surprising variety. Compare them with the one your child made.

45 Transportation, Traffic, and Highways

When I was a child, the New Jersey Turnpike was completed, and my parents and I drove all the way up from Baltimore to take a ride. When I tell my children that we once drove the Jersey Pike for fun, they find it hard to believe.

You'll Need various ways of getting around; a familiar road; community resources; paper and pencils

Before You Begin Give your child the experience of getting around in all sorts of ways: streetcars, buses, subways (in the front car, where he can see the tunnel), taxicabs, all kinds of cars, as well as on horseback, in horse and buggy, and even on foot.

What to Do

1 Ask your child, "What do you think is under this road?" Entertain all suggestions with interest and respect. Talk about each of them to understand your child's thinking on the subject. "Why do you think there's dirt under the road . . . or cobblestones . . . or train tracks . . . or another, older road?" Ask your child to try to imagine what the area was like before the road was built.

2 Look for clues along the road to get new ideas about what the area might have been like. Check potholes and curbstones, as well as things along the side of the road, such as old houses, old fences, stone walls, or hitching posts.

3 Get help from other people in your community. Ask an older person or someone who is knowledgeable about your area to describe how people got around years ago. Was this

road here? Was another road here? If possible, go to a local library or government office to search out maps, bus routes, and the like.

Follow-up Activities
- Have your child draw a picture of what your road might have looked like long ago.
- Search your community for old stuff—lithographs, maps, photographs, stories—that show what life was like for people back then.

What's Happening Here are some of the things a friend has found out by doing this activity with her children over the years: Her home is built on what was once an orchard, the park down the street was built after a hat factory on the site was leveled as hats went out of fashion, the road covers trolley tracks that once ran from the hat factory to residential areas in other towns, the rest of the street was a dirt road and the sidewalks were dirt paths, the brook down the street was once dammed for an ice-skating pond, and someone fell through the ice who has the same name as one of the streets that turns off her road. You can see how this activity opens doors to real lives—and ways of life—in the past.

Moving Ahead When you're planning your next vacation and discussing transportation with your child, consider together how people would have gotten there years before.

Helpful Hint Read:
- *The Little House* by Virgina Lee Burton (Houghton Mifflin, 1978)
- *Under the Moon* by Dyan Sheldon (Dial, 1994)

PART FOUR

Eyes, Ears, Body, and Soul

The goal of this section is to explore some of the ways that people fulfill their basic need for self-expression. These music, art, dance, celebration, decoration, and drama activities are for you and your child to enjoy together and with anyone—and everyone—with whom you can get involved.

46 Postcards from the Masters

*The idea is not to equip your child to identify
Picassos and van Goghs, but to help her to enjoy them
from the heart and to notice mood and expression
as communicated by different artists.*

You'll Need an art museum; an assortment of art postcards; painting supplies

Before You Begin Visit an art museum and bring home a bag of art postcards.

What to Do

1 First, offer the cards to your child as something to look at, play with, sort, and explore.

2 After your child has had some time to play with the cards on her own, ask, "Which two cards do you think are alike?" No matter which two your child picks, your next question is the same: "What's alike about them?" Listen. Focus on what your child says.

3 Now you pick two cards. Talk about what is alike about them, what they have in common. Talk about how you think the works were painted. Focus on things your child can see, such as technique, color, line, or design, rather than time periods, names of artists, or schools of art.

Follow-up Activities

- Pick a card, and take your child to the museum to look at that painting. Now's the time to talk about the painting and who made it, to put a face with the painting.

- Encourage your child to pick a card and look through the pile for another painting that appears to have been painted by the same person. Talk about your child's reason for her choice.

- Paint with your child.

What's Happening　Through this activity, your child becomes familiar with wonderful art and comfortable with noting its features and attributes, in comparing one artist or style with another, in gathering the cards into groups. Through informal research in my school, I've observed that children doing art-work in classrooms with impressionist pictures displayed on the walls begin painting like impressionists. When the painting style is changed to cubism, their artwork takes on a cubist cast. If children can feast their eyes on a variety of artwork—and therefore on a variety of representations of the world—then they will develop flexibility in their own attitude toward art.

Moving Ahead　Once your child is familiar with your selection of cards, you can begin focusing on individual artists and schools. Use your cards to create a timeline of artistic ideas, working with your child over time to find out all you can about what painters were thinking or trying to show in their work.

Helpful Hint　It's a good idea to get postcards from a museum, but if there's nothing close by, search out reproductions of paintings in cat-alogs and magazines, or look for the game Art Cards by Aristoplay, Ltd.

47 You Could Have Been in Pictures

Helps develop: understanding of composition in painting; awareness of drama, color, mood, and feeling

Be your own painting!

You'll Need a museum; a box of costumes of any kind (old clothes are just right); the biggest empty picture frame you can find (rummage sales and junk shops are a good source); 2 chairs; a large mirror; other children, props, or child-painted backdrop (optional); camera (Polaroid works well, so your child can see his portrait right away)

Before You Begin Take your child to a museum and show him paintings of people, or share a book of reproductions of paintings with your child.

What to Do
1 Invite your child to dress up in any costume that pleases him.
2 Prop two sides of the picture frame against the backs of two chairs.
3 Position the mirror opposite the frame so that when your child stands behind the frame and looks out, he can see himself.
4 Invite your child to "be a painting" by standing in costume behind the picture frame. Encourage other children to join him. Add props and even a child-painted backdrop.
5 Record the moment with your camera.

Follow-up Activities
- Invite your child to "be" other paintings, and take a picture of each setup.
- Display all your photos. Talk with your child about all the different ways one subject can look in various pictures.
- Suggest that your child try painting a picture that looks like one of the setups.

Your child is experimenting with a number of things: his own appearance, the composition of an image within a given space and shape, and an understanding of subject, positioning, props, and background. What's more, he's gaining insight into some of the processes an artist goes through when making a painting. You can use this activity as a springboard for discussions of models, studios, and other practical points about painting.

Moving Ahead Encourage your child and other children with him to mimic real paintings. They can dress up as people in paintings and position themselves as the people appear, wearing similar expressions and attitudes. Later, match the photographs you took with the paintings they're based on.

Helpful Hint Read *The Gentleman and the Kitchen Maid* by Diane Stanley (Dial, 1994), a delightful story about the relationships between the people in the paintings in one room of an art museum.

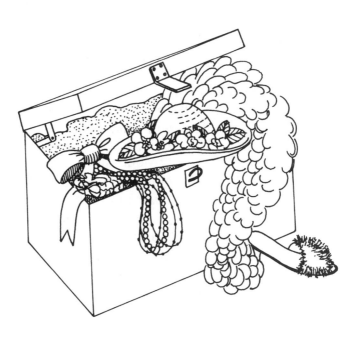

48 For the Love of Michelangelo (or Any Other Artist)

Expose your child to art. Let her pick somebody to follow. Then go the whole route, following your child's lead.

You'll Need art books (for adults and/or children) from library or art museum; art postcards and other reproductions of artwork; painting and sculpturing supplies; history books

Before You Begin Talk with your child about different artists and their work. Notice when she seems particularly interested in one artist.

What to Do 1 Pinpoint an artist in whom your child shows a strong interest. Some possibilities:

- Your child is wild about a specific painting. (I know one four-year-old who was mad for *Broadway Boogie Woogie* by Mondrian.)
- Your child reads a book about an artist *(Linnea in Monet's Garden).*
- Your child loves mobiles (such as those by Alexander Calder).
- Your child sees a photograph of Matisse making tissue cutouts and thinks it's cool that his floor is so messy.

2 Invite your child to learn more about this artist's life. Look for library books, museum displays, and other sources that provide pictures and stories.

3 Take your child in search of artwork by this person. Art books are a great excuse to include your child in a search at

an adult library, and the books themselves are wonderful to share with your child—they're gorgeous to look at and awesome in their feel, smell, and heft.

4 Provide your child with postcards or other reproductions of the artist's artwork.

5 Talk to your child about the artist's life. How does his or her personality, environment, and the things that happened to the artist come through the paintings?

Follow-up Activities
- Have your child make or paint something that mimics the artist's technique. This is especially helpful with three-dimensional art like sculpture and mobiles.
- Read history books with your child to find out what life was like during the artist's time.

What's Happening *Your child is plucking one rose out of the garden for closer examination. Through this activity you encourage your child to explore, enjoy, and dissect one person's artwork, and to find out everything she can about this real person's daily life and outlook. As with anyone in history, finding out what things were like for that person provides history hooks for the imagination to hang facts on. Art history, typically an adult realm, is especially attractive to children, who can easily understand the need to express oneself through the hands, and who are fascinated by the story behind every picture.*

Moving Ahead Encourage your child to study illustrators as well—true fine artists whose work is probably already on display in your home, school, and children's library. Some favorites: Maurice Sendak, Chris Van Allsburg, Trina Schart Hyman, Steven Kellogg, and Leo and Diane Dillon.

Helpful Hint Here are some adult books to help you help your child:
- *Mommy, It's a Renoir* by Aline Wolf (Parent Child Press, 1984)
- *Doing Art Together* by Muriel Silbertstein-Storfer with Mablen Jones (Simon & Schuster, 1982)

. . . and some books for your child to enjoy:
- *Linnea in Monet's Garden* by Christina Bjork (Farrar, Straus & Giroux, 1987)
- *Roarr! Calder's Circus* by Maira Kalman (Doubleday, 1993)

49 Paint Your Own Walls

Why do kids—and why did cave dwellers—draw on walls?

You'll Need a wall; paint and paintbrushes or markers *or* butcher paper or large sheets of white paper; thumbtacks or tape (if using paper); newspapers or drop cloth; paper towels; camera (optional); smock

Before You Begin Choose a wall that you feel comfortable making available to your child.

What to Do

1 Invite your child to decorate a wall with paint or markers. Encourage him to choose paint colors and brushes.

2 Set things up with your child. If you're going to have him paint directly on the wall, talk to him about it first. Let him know that the paint job he does here will be relatively permanent. Ask him to consider what he'll paint before he starts. (However, with most water-based paint, you can wipe it off with a wet paper towel if things are really disappointing or "wrong.") If you're not painting the wall, tack or

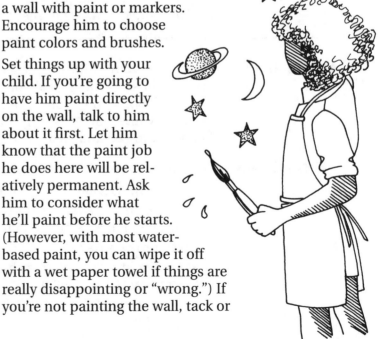

tape up large sheets of paper, but be sure it's thick enough that the paint won't seep through.

3 Cover the floor with newspapers or a drop cloth. Set up the paint and brushes. Provide paper towels (some of which are damp) for cleanup or to wipe away "mistakes."

4 Let your painter go to town!

5 Involve the artist in cleaning up. Admire the newly painted wall!

Follow-up Activities

- Take a picture of your child with his artwork so that he can better understand scale and the idea of reproduced (rather than original) art.

- Invite your child to repaint the wall periodically.

What's Happening

Through letting your child express himself on the wall, you affirm his individuality, his artistic ability, and his ability to be careful and to work through the process of creating a work of art. Self-expression is a basic human need. Through talking, singing, dancing, or doing art, people of all ages and all periods in history show what matters most to them. House-proud parents should be family-proud first. Let your house speak for your whole family, not for just a few of you.

Moving Ahead

Pick up some of the many wonderful art projects on the market that allow your child to decorate his own clothing, make his own jewelry, or create his own anything. Encourage your child to express himself in this way, and then wear it, use it, display it.

Helpful Hint

An alternative to paint is strippable wallpaper in solid colors that serves as a canvas for felt-tipped markers.

50 The Silence Game

Helps develop: abilities to concentrate, relax, study something, and listen closely

It's important for kids to be able to hear silence.

You'll Need an art object—something pretty to look at (a vase of flowers, for example); candle (optional); soft music (optional)

Before You Begin Find time to be quiet together with your child.

What to Do

1 Tell your child that you're going to get quiet together and look at something so that she and you can hear better.

2 Get very comfortable. Put an art object where you can both see it easily. You might even light a candle to add to the specialness of the mood you're creating.

3 Tell your child in a quiet voice to breathe in and out slowly. Invite her to look at the object and to think of it in silence.

4 In a quieter voice, tell your child to continue to relax, breathe in and out, listen to her heartbeat, to her breathing. Tell her that later you'll talk about the things she can hear in the room, in the house, outside.

5 Become silent. Together, sit and look and listen.

6 After a few minutes, begin to talk not necessarily in a whisper.

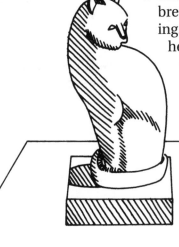

- Talk about the things you heard and how you both feel.
- Try this activity on other occasions, increasing the time.
- Try this activity outside.
- Add some soft New Age music or recordings of whales' songs.

What's Happening

This game (a kind of meditation) is a way to help your child center herself, to pull a sense of quietness into her body. It is extremely important for children who are always on the go and often visually focused to learn to focus on what they can hear. All children benefit from being able to hear silence (even if it's not really silent where you live). This game is good for on-the-go mothers and fathers as well.

Moving Ahead

Encourage your child to initiate her own Silence Game with you when she feels she needs a quiet, relaxing moment.

Helpful Hint

Many of us who have experienced childbirth know breathing, focusing, and concentration techniques that can help control and relax our bodies and our minds. Share your own tricks for calming down with your child.

51 Body Music

Helps develop:
rhythm, under-
standing of sound's
properties and
variations

*Everybody could make the rich variety of sounds
that Bobby McFerrin makes—if only they 'd stop, slow down,
listen, experiment, invent, create, practice, explore . . . .*

You'll Need you and your child

Before You Begin Pay attention to the noises your child makes.

What to Do

1 The next time your child makes a simple noise—a clap, a burp, a hum—say, "Hey, that's an interesting sound you're making. How do you do that?" Encourage your child to demonstrate how it's done.

2 Try making the sound yourself. Ask, "Does it sound the same when I do it?" Ask why or why not.

3 Have your child make the sound again. Try holding your hands over his ears as he makes the noise, then release your hands. Ask, "Did that make it sound different?"

4 Invite your child to take turns making the sound with you. Together, work out a rhythm that involves each of you making the sound solo, then both together.

Follow-up Activities

- Develop new sounds in the same way. Try finger snapping, belly slapping, foot stomping, toe tapping, and so on.
- Imitate the sounds things make, as a variation on charades. Imitate animals, machines, musical instruments.
- Talk about what makes each sound, and what makes each sound different.

Through this activity you open the door to a whole world of sounds that can be made very simply by using the body on its own or against other objects, including itself. As you play with your child, creating noises and melodies from sounds, he explores tone, rhythm, pitch, and other qualities. You can also help him focus on the role position plays in sound by comparing the sounds your child makes and hears inside his head to the same sounds made by you.

Moving Ahead   Record body sounds and then encourage your child to try to identify them by listening.

Helpful Hint   For original body and mouth noises, nobody rivals Bobby McFerrin, a fun-loving, talented, classically trained musician. Try this tape:

- *Hush* with Bobby McFerrin and Yo-Yo Ma (Sony Classical)

52 Opera around the House

Helps develop:
appreciation of
music as a form of
self-expression,
language concepts

*If you're of a certain generation, you're likely to burst into
a certain song anytime you find yourself on a hilltop—a song
sung by Julie Andrews in* The Sound of Music. *That's opera:
taking an emotion and turning it into a song.*

You'll Need   various kinds of music

Before You Begin   Play all kinds of music for your child.

What to Do   **1** One day as you're folding the underwear, flipping ham-
burgers, pushing your child on a swing, start singing about
it. "One underwear, two underwear, three underwear, four."
Don't worry about sounding operatic—that's not the point
here. The point is to sing about what you're doing, thinking,
and feeling.

2 Encourage your child to join in. One way to do this is to
ask a question in song. "Do you want me to push you
hi-i-i-igher?" Comply only if your child replies in song.

3 Hold an entire conversation in song.

Follow-up Activities   • Talk about opera as an art form—a play in which people
sing all the words.

• Mix into your opera songs you and your child already know
by linking them to conversation. For example, you could
look outside and comment (in song) that it's snowing, then
sing "Frosty the Snowman."

Too often opera is presented to children (and adults) as something they should know about or do in order to be "cultured" or "classy." How did it ever get such a reputation? In its original form, opera was the people's entertainment, full of excitement, a thrill a minute, with colorful performers and sets. Your child can see opera that way if she begins learning about it by doing it, with only minimal focus on musical or vocal quality. Those of us who grew up warbling "I want my Rice Krispies" or "The hills are alive" know just how much fun opera—in its simplest form—can be.

Moving Ahead

Watch opera on television or video. Watch brief portions, and talk about what the people seem to be saying and feeling. It helps to use operas written or performed in English. Note that they don't have to be complete operas or classical operas. Check out portions of *Tommy, Candide,* or *The Pirates of Penzance.*

Helpful Hint

- Look for operas performed as part of *Mister Rogers' Neighborhood.*

- Try *Mozart's Magic Fantasy: A Journey through "The Magic Flute"* (Classical Kids, 1990), a beautiful dramatization (in English) written especially for young children.

53 Cab Calloway

Helps develop:
*listening skills,
rhythm, relationship
between words and
music, memory*

*He was the Hi-de-ho man, who called out a chant
for the audience to repeat. Much loved and much imitated,
Cab Calloway is the inspiration for this activity.*

You'll Need   catchy phrase, such as a line from a Cab Calloway recording

Before You Begin   Use a Cab Calloway line, or any catchy phrase or tongue-twister, to start you on this activity.

What to Do   **1** Play Echo with your child. Ask him to listen to you and repeat what you say. Begin with a one-word chant. Have your child echo one word at a time.

Hey.   (Hey.)

Ho.   (Ho.)

Hi.   (Hi.)

Who.   (Who.)

You.   (You.)

Me.   (Me.)

They.   (They.)

Hey!   (Hey!)

2 Work from one word to two words and then three or more.

One.   (One.)

One two.   (One two.)

One two three.   (One two three.)

One two three hop.   (One two three hop.)

One two three jump.   (One two three jump.)

One two three go!   (One two three go!)

3 Invite your child to start the chant and you be the echo.

Follow-up Activity   Sing songs that have echoes and responses. Here are some favorite examples. See Helpful Hints for others.

- "Rudolph, the Red-Nosed Reindeer" with responses (ask a grade-schooler to sing it for you)
- "The Other Day I Saw a Bear"
- "Rise and Shine"

What's Happening   Most children can sing, but not all can sing with other people. Singing as an echo is a discipline that requires listening, recalling, and repeating. Echoing is fun, it's a cooperative effort, and it produces a beautiful sound.

Moving Ahead   Encourage your child to listen for songs with echoes in them while you play the radio or a tape.

Helpful Hints

- *Rise Up Singing* (Sing Out Corporation, 1988) is an excellent source of all kinds of songs, including many echo songs. It includes guitar chords and information about the recordings.
- Check Cab Calloway recordings for these echo-chant songs, among others:
    "Fifteen-Minute Intermission"
    "The Calloway Boogie"
    "Hi-De-Ho Man"
- Read *Yo! Yes?* by Chris Raschka (Orchard Books, 1993).

54 Your Own Music Curriculum

*H**elps develop:**
flexibility in
thinking about music;
understanding of
styles, patterns,
rhythms*

*Just as with food, clothing, and shelter types, children
need to learn about different kinds of music in order
to develop an appreciation and respect for many
cultures, time periods, and other people's tastes.*

You'll Need
recordings and/or performances of many different kinds of
music; tape recorder (optional)

Before You Begin
Introduce your child to a variety of music styles. Play music at
all different times.

What to Do
1 Play a piece of music for your child. Encourage her to listen
in her own way, in any position she wants, while doing any
activity she wants. (That way music becomes part of everyday life, not something she needs to sit down and study.)

2 Talk about the music your child hears.

3 Ask her for suggestions of what tape or CD to play next.
Discuss what she likes or doesn't like, what the music has in
common with other music styles, what the instruments
sound like.

4 Imitate the music you hear with your child. "Can you make
that high oboe sound?" "Can you sound as happy as that
trumpet?"

Follow-up Activities
• Seek out free or admission-charged performances and con-
certs of many types of music. Take your child along. Let her
know if you don't know what to expect. Together, compare
the music you hear with other music you've heard in the
past.

• Borrow recordings from friends or music libraries.

• Encourage your child to tape her favorite music for a friend.

Children who grow up hearing opera may not love opera all their lives, but they'll know what it's all about. Children who grow up hearing Duke Ellington will have a solid feeling of what jazz is all about. It's to your child's benefit to expose her to as many different kinds of music as possible, defining each style with just that word: different. Go ahead and teach your child all the words to the Beatles' songs, if those are your favorites. Make a point, also, of giving her music from other countries, cultures, and times, and of letting her hear as many different instruments and voices as possible.

Moving Ahead

Use music to create a history timeline. Gather together an assortment of recordings from various time periods, and work with your child to put them in chronological order. If you can, relate each piece of music to what was going on in the music world at that time, and, as important, what was going on in the world at large. Connect music with other history hooks from timelines you made in Activity 7: History Hooks or Activity 14: One Moment in Time.

Helpful Hints

Music for Little People, whose products are available through mail order and retail, is a source of music recordings from many different cultures and times. Check also:

- *The Laura Ingalls Wilder Songbook* edited by Eugenia Garson (HarperCollins, 1968)
- *The Raffi Everything Grows Songbook* (Crown, 1989)
- *The Kidz Family Car Songbook* (Running Press, 1991)

55 Your Songs

Helps develop: basics of musical notation, association between sung and written language

A friend was rocking her two-year-old one day, when the child sat up and said, "Mom, don't sing that song!" "Why not?" responded the mother. "I always sing that to you!" "Yes," said the child, "and I don't like it." "Didn't you ever like it?" said the mother. "No!"

You'll Need many different kinds of music to listen to; musical instrument (optional); a cassette tape recorder and tape; sketchbook; pencils, crayons, or markers

Before You Begin Encourage your child to listen to many different kinds of music.

What to Do

1 Invite your child to work with you to make a tape-and-book set of his favorite songs. Ask him to list the songs for you and to plan which one should go first, second, and so on.

2 Help your child rehearse his songs. Include accompaniment, if you want, on piano, tambourine, guitar, or any other instrument.

3 Tape your child singing.

4 Play the tape and make revisions if your child thinks they're necessary. As he listens, ask him to think about the words and what they mean.

5 Have your child use the sketchbook to draw a picture to go with each song. Suggest that your child write each song in invented writing. (Provide no guidance here. Encourage your child to come up with his own way of representing written language and/or musical notes and directions.)

Follow-up Activities

• Invite your child to play his tape and to look through his book with you or with a friend.

• Encourage your child to add more songs to his tape and book if he wants or to make new versions at other times.

What's Happening   You're doing a number of valuable things in this activity. You're working through the process of planning, rehearsing, recording, and editing a tape with your child, helping him to see and act through all the steps. Through creating artwork, your child connects images with music. Through writing down musical notation in any way he sees fit, your child gets an early and basic understanding of music as a different kind of language. Later, you can introduce him to the idea of standard musical notation, saying something like, "This is how some people write down music."

Moving Ahead   Your child may be interested to see how his interest in music changes over time. Keep his tapes and books on hand for future comparisons. You can share your own music collection as well, talking to your child about the way your taste in music has evolved over the years.

Helpful Hint   Make a book of songs that the whole family likes to sing, and a tape to go with it. This can be a good way to teach tolerance, respect for taste, and differences in musical styles.

56 Make Me a Mirror

56 Make Me
a Mirror

Helps develop: memory, awareness of pattern, coordination between thought and action, self-esteem, leadership

This deceptively simple game can bring out many wonderful things in your child—and in your relationship with her.

You'll Need mirror

Before You Begin Encourage your child to look at herself in the mirror as she brushes her teeth, combs her hair, and so on, and to watch her movements.

What to Do

1 Stand in front of a mirror. Ask your child to watch what the mirror does when you move. Tell her that you're going to play a game without the real mirror that involves one person being the Mover and the other being the Mirror.

2 Invite your child to choose whether she wants to be the Mover or the Mirror.

3 The Mover stands facing the Mirror, about 2 feet (⅔ m) away. The Mover starts by slowly moving hands, head, and so on while standing in place, just as a person would have to do in front of a real mirror. The Mirror reflects the Mover's actions, moving left hand to match right, and so on.

Follow-up Activities

- Switch roles.
- Try together to increase your ability to mirror each other faster. The shorter the response time, the better the team works together.

What's Happening

When your child is the Mirror, she has to watch closely and anticipate your movements in order to most closely reflect them. When she is the Mover, she can try to surprise the Mirror with unexpected actions, or she can slow down to orchestrate a smooth performance in which an audience can't tell who is the Mirror and who is the Mover.

Moving Ahead

When you're the Mover, reach a hand toward the Mirror. Help your child to see where the Mover should stop and the "glass" of the Mirror begin. Go on from this activity to other ones that involve mime, inviting your child to playact peeling a banana, putting on shoes, or doing some other everyday activity without the benefit of props or speech.

Helpful Hint

Try playing this game with and without talking. Which is easier? Why?

57 Make Your Own Special Effects

Make Your Own
Special Effects

Helps develop:
critical thinking,
problem-solving
skills

Look, Mom!
It's the two-headed alien dog from Mars!

You'll Need tabloid cover; construction paper or newsprint; camera; scissors; glue stick; pencil; newspaper; computer with newspaper-style font (optional)

Before You Begin Take your child to the grocery store and let him look at all the magazines and tabloids for sale at the checkout counter.

What to Do 1 When your child asks a question about the weird specimen pictured on the cover of a tabloid, turn the question around. "What do you think? . . . It says, 'two-headed dog.' How could that be? . . . I wonder how they made the picture look like that."

2 Read the headline to your child (unless it's wildly inappropriate, which is often the case). Talk to your child about why a newspaper might want to print wild stories and impossible photographs.

3 Invite your child to create her own tabloid cover on construction paper or newsprint. What would she want the picture to show? How could such a picture be made? For example, if she really wants to show a two-headed dog, take pictures of your dog in two different positions, have your child cut the head from one picture and add it to the other, then take a new picture of the combined picture. Have your child glue the new picture on the paper.

4 Help your child come up with a suitable headline, and have her write it on her cover in invented writing. Or find the words in real newspapers, cut them out, and paste them

TWO-HEADED DOG SIGHTED!!!

on. If you have a computer, your child can type her head-line in a newspaper-style font, print it out, and glue it on her cover.

Follow-up Activity Together, think of other laughable "news" from your house-hold and publish it in your child's newspaper.

What's Happening Through this activity, you're demystifying the process of putting together a newspaper (or tabloid). At the same time, you're introducing the concept of special effects—an important awareness for any child in this day and age to have—and helping your child to gain an understanding of how they're done. Your child will come to understand that exaggeration—hyperbole—grabs people's attention but is often disappointing when the real story is revealed.

Moving Ahead Television, movies, magazines, and advertising are chock-full of special effects. Wonder with your child about each of these media and try to figure out together how the effects are done.

Helpful Hint Look through books of photographs with your child. Enjoy them together, and use them as a springboard for a discussion of what each photographer chose to show—and to omit.

58 Superhero

Who is that masked woman?

You'll Need   superhero costume stuff (cape, mask, helmet, shield, sword, etc.—from materials on hand or improvised by your child); paper and pencil (optional); other children

Before You Begin   Get your child talking about the current superhero craze, those plastic figures that show up on so many wish lists and occupy so much space in toy stores. Ask your child to tell you what the superheroes can do (and how), who they are in "real life," what they wear, what they say, and why they're "cool."

What to Do

1 Invite your child to invent her own superhero, someone she can dress up as and pretend to be. Ask, "What should you (the superhero) be able to do? Why? How?" In this discussion, you can cover issues such as good guys and bad guys, ammunition and defense, magic words and powers, costumes, and so on.

2 Make a plan with your child to equip her in the costume she needs. Encourage her to use stuff around the house to transform herself. As she works, suggest that your child think of a name for her superhero—and maybe also one for the superhero's workaday alias.

3 Play Superhero together. Let her "save" you in her costume.

Follow-up Activities

• Encourage your child to playact and/or write stories about herself as a superhero.

• Involve friends or siblings in the act. What characters can they be? Work together to create scenarios involving your child as the superhero.

Instead of just mouthing lore about plastic or television characters, your child puts together what she knows about superheroes to invent her own—and to reinvent herself. In doing so, she realizes what goes into creating a superhero, and transfers the superhero character to herself. This doesn't mean that children shouldn't play with this kind of toy or develop scenarios around commercial toys, but that it's important for kids to see the mind behind the magic, and to understand that power doesn't lie only in what's popularized on television.

Moving Ahead   With your child, read stories about historical figures who are heroes, and also about mythological heroes. Your child may notice commonalties between present-day superheroes and the gods and goddesses of Greece, Rome, or the Nordic countries.

Helpful Hint   Stories about superheroes include these:

- *Tell Me a Trudy* by Lore Segal (Farrar, Straus & Giroux, 1977)
- *Kat Kong and Dogzilla* by Dav Pilkey (Harcourt Brace, 1993)

59 Modeling Play

Helps develop:
*dramatic sense,
empathy, critical
thinking*

If at first you don't succeed, mash it and start again.

You'll Need   modeling clay; paint or crayons; white paper; scissors; shoe box or other medium-size box; camera and bookmaking materials (optional)

Before You Begin   If possible, take your child to see a puppet show.

What to Do   **1** Invite your child to work with you to create a puppet play.

2 Let your child use modeling clay to make puppets. Explain to your child that modeling clay is flexible—if he wants to change his puppet, he can.

3 Together, think of a story for the puppets to playact. What will happen to them? How will they feel? Practice the story together a few times.

4 Talk about the story's setting. Where will the story take place? Use paint or crayons to create a paper backdrop for each scene.

5 Cut out the bottom of a shoe box to make a stage for the puppets to act in. Stand the box on one long side on a tabletop, and hang the paper backdrop on a wall behind the stage. You and your child kneel behind the table to operate the puppets.

6 Perform the puppet play with your child.

Follow-up Activities   • Help your child to photograph each scene and use the photographs to create a picture book that tells the story of his puppet play.

• Use the modeling-clay figures to introduce your child to animation. Take pictures of the clay figures, changing or moving them slightly from one photo to the next, until you have a sequence of pictures. Then quickly flip the pictures to show how they simulate motion.

Through puppet play, your child has the opportunity to act out scenarios that are important to him. He can say and feel and do things through the puppet that he might not feel empowered to do on his own. When your child makes his own puppets, you increase the medium's natural potential for drama and flexibility, and make it even more personal for your child. Making puppets of clay takes away worry about not getting things right. With clay, things can always be mashed and rebuilt.

Moving Ahead   Save or remake favorite characters. Use them—and the scenes they appear in—as the basis for a book. Your child can draw or paint pictures showing the characters, and use invented writing to write a script to go with them.

Helpful Hint   Sculpey, available in most toy and crafts stores, is a great invention—it's a polymer that can be modeled like clay, baked to hardness, and kept.

60 Pants Pillow

Helps develop:
problem-solving
skills, recycling
sensibility

Say! Didn't that pillow used to be . . . ?

You'll Need   an old, outgrown pair of pants; scissors; pins; needles and thread *or* sewing machine; stuffing material—old, outgrown socks or T-shirts work well (cut the T-shirts up); fabric paints or markers (optional); other old clothes

Before You Begin   Talk with your child about ways that things become new by being used in new ways: a smooth beach rock becomes a paperweight; a worn-thin towel or sweater becomes a bed for the cat; an old bottle becomes a vase or a candleholder. Introduce your child to the idea "It's old, but it's new to me!"

What to Do   1 Invite your child to help you find a way to use an old pair of pants to make a pillow for the bed or a cushion for the floor. Lay the pants out flat on the floor or table, and take a good look at them. Ask your child, "How could we cut the pants to get a square pillow? A short rectangular pillow? A long bolster?"

2 Cut the pants at the knee or the top of the thigh to get the shape you want. You can make a square pillow from the hip section of the pants, a short rectangular pillow out of a half leg, and a bolster out of a whole leg.

3 Ask your child to help you sew, stuff, and close the pillow.

Follow-up Activities   • Have your child decorate the pillow with fabric paints or markers.

• Find ways to make pillows out of T-shirts, skirts, or other clothing.

• Figure out other things to make from old clothes: a wig with braids from an old pair of tights, a drawstring handbag out of a pair of shorts (sew the legs shut), and whatever else you can think of.

What's Happening *Giving up old clothes can be a wrenching problem to some children. By helping your child find a way to keep a loved object close at hand, you demonstrate respect for and understanding of both material value and personal values. In this materialistic society, it is easy for children to learn that the best things are new and shiny. A child who learns to make a pillow from a favorite article of old clothing learns that growth means positive change, that problems can be solved in many ways, and that materials have many possible uses and boundless potential.*

Moving Ahead Encourage your child to search out interesting objects in junk shops or in Salvation Army stores. Talk about where each object might have come from, how old it is, how it was made (and of what materials), and who might have owned it.

Helpful Hint Keep an eye out for new things made from old goods: park benches made from recycled milk bottles, sculptures made from scrap, birdfeeders made from bleach bottles, etc.

Activities Index

About the Authors

Marlene Barron is an internationally known educator and authority on the educational and developmental needs of preschool and elementary school children. She holds a Ph.D. in Early Childhood and Elementary Education. Her focus is early literacy development. She is Head of West Side Montessori School in New York City and a professor at New York University. Dr. Barron gives frequent lectures and workshops on early childhood education around the country and also publishes articles in professional journals. She is the author of *I Learn to Read and Write the Way I Learn to Talk: A Very First Book About Whole Language.*

Karen Romano Young is a writer specializing in educational materials for children, teachers, and parents. Formerly an editor at Scholastic, she has written for the National Geographic Society and Children's Television Workshop. Her work has appeared in books, magazines, and other media. Ms. Young holds a B.S. in elementary education and is the mother of three children.